UNLIKELY PASSAGES

UNLIKELY PASSAGES

by Reese Palley

SHERIDAN HOUSE

This edition published 1998 by
Sheridan House Inc.
145 Palisade Street
Dobbs Ferry, NY 10522

Library of Congress Cataloging-in-Publication Data

Palley, Reese.
    Unlikely passages / by Reese Palley
       p.   cm.
    Originally published: Newport, R.I. : Seven Seas Press. c1984
    ISBN 1-57409-051-8 (alk. paper)
    1. Sailing—Humor.   I. Title.
    GV811.P28 1998
    797. 1'24'0207—dc21   97-52028
                                       CIP

Design by Irving Perkins Associates

Printed in the United States of America

ISBN   1-57409-051-8

Foreword to the Paperback Edition

The other day I went to a book sale in our home town library of Key West. There were thousands of abandoned books, some by the best of authors, some ephemera on subjects of the moment, some coffee table and art books, history books and so on. I became transfixed at the sheer volume of all of this castaway effort.

I was dizzied by them. I could reach in any direction and put my hand on books which touched my heart and mind as they had touched thousands of readers when they were first published. Now they were twenty-five cents...some as much as a dollar. Few would be read again. What effort. What waste.

A few days after the sale, my publisher, Lothar Simon of Sheridan House, called with the startling request that, after thirteen years, he wanted to reprint *Unlikely Passages*. From among the Niagara of books that lay dying on shelves, Lothar wanted to give life again to this one. I was enormously flattered.

Unlikely Passages has had a curious history. It was brought out by Seven Seas Press in 1984. Seven Seas shortly thereafter, and I pray not because of my book, went belly up. *Unlikely Passages*, after a surprisingly strong acceptance, was thus orphaned off before it ever got out of kindergarten.

Some thousands of copies were remaindered, at a penny a pound, to an anonymous warehouse for dead books. In an hubric gesture of authorial pride, I bought them all.

But books have a life of their own, unrelated to the financial fortunes of their publishers. I began to receive inquiries for the book. It quickly assumed cult status, and, handed from one reader to the next, clung to a life granted by readers who refused to let it die. For over a decade I fed the few copies I had to sailors all over the world. It had touched a nerve.

Given the opportunity to rewrite and correct some really embarrassing errors, I chose to change nothing. I hold that error is a necessary factor of the creative process. Since I believe that life follows art, the writing, errors and all, stands.

By way of dedication, I stand grateful to the sailors who remembered *Unlikely Passages* in their hearts. I stand endlessly impressed with Jim Gilbert who editorially wrought the book into its final shape and to Lothar Simon who found the need to republish it. But, most of all I am grateful to my wife Marilyn who has always insisted that I keep writing and that I keep the faith.

Unlikely Passages now starts out on this second passage of its own, accompanied by my deepest desire that it might give a new audience a little giggle.

For, in truth, that is all it was ever meant to do.

Reese Palley
Key West, November 1997

I hereby acknowledge these unrepayable debts:

To Bella Alexander for nurturing.
To Gloria Romanelli for forcing me to buy *Unlikely V*
and for a number of other things.
To Kathy Quinn, Attorney and Literata, for teaching
me the rigors of writing.
To Marilyn Arnold, Weaver, who read and suffered
through every unedited word.
To Andrea Sirlin, Songmaker, who first insisted that
these scribblings were a book and to Irving for
looking after her.
To Dr. Roy Ritts, A Very Smart Man, who almost
succumbed to the disease of Terminal Prolix.
To Marcus Rizzardini and Cyndee Horner, Sailors, without
whom any passage would be unthinkable.
To Alan Werkesman, Attorney, for his affirmation when
affirmation was desperately needed.
To Jim Gilbert, Editor Born, who took a mélange de jeunesse
and wrought a book.
And to Norman Palley, Brother, without whom life would be
considerably less worth living.

CONTENTS

— Prologue —

An Encouragement Of Ancients

We are born struggling against the simple obligation to breathe. Immediately we begin reinventing the wheels of relationship with those around us. We learn first to identify our mother (easy, she has the nipple) and thence forward and outward into the bewildering, infinitely expanding universe of blood relationships. Our fathers and our cousins and our sisters and our aunts have little meaning to us since they seem to be absent of nipples. And all this before we are barely a year old.

In this first 12 months of existence we learn we must carefully prepare ourselves for the second 12 months. And in the second, for the third, and the third the fourth and so on until, upon completing our formal education, we realize all this preparation has been aimed at enabling us to feed ourselves and making it possible to avoid boredom in the approaching years of adulthood.

Our society, our genes and our uncontrollable chemistry conspire throughout our unconscious immaturity, to prepare us to be of some undefined use to the world. We learn the habit of preparation, of getting ready to do that "wonderful thing" for ourselves and our world.

For some of us that wonderful thing is simply a family,

as satisfying as was the Bomb for Oppenheimer. Some of us make what an old rabbi friend called "a permanent contribution," unalterably altering society, affecting an unquenchable genetic twist, or, taking a moment of someone else's poetry, making a footprint in the sandy loam of history.

These works, good and bad, all start with preparation. Find the nipple so you can suck, suck so you can grow, grow so you can learn and thus be prepared, like Boy Scouts, to pleasurably live out your adultage.

So what about our dotage? How come the process halts for our silver locks and golden years? Why does age come upon us as such a damned surprise, so unlike the advent of adulthood, which was endlessly planned for, anticipated, manipulated? If we can spend the first five years getting ready for Kindergarten should we not be allowed, if not forced, to spend some of the ensuing fifty preparing for Altengarten?

Unless you are unlucky in that great genetic lottery in the sky, you can go on physically and emotionally, with little qualitative degradation, until some jealous husband or errant wisp of industrial waste lays you low. If your genes are good you can screw until doomsday and leave behind a brood who can, in their turn, screw until doomsday. If you like to see form in stone you may, as Jacques Lipschitz wished for, remain toujours verde, chipping away the excess, until, as your century approaches, you topple dizzily off a forty-foot scaffold to an honorable artist's death. If you crave physical adventure you may, like that other Jacques, the venerable Cousteau, open a watery universe new to man, absorbing in the process the defenses against age of the undying carp. If you like to write, and if you have something to say, look about at the scribbling Ancients who go on writing long after you have forgotten how to read.

You all know these accomplished Ancients. Perhaps there is one around the corner from you, or in your own living room? Or, if you are lucky, you may have one in your own bedroom.

Escape from artificially-imposed senility happens to too few. The crystal laws of chance say there should be more escapes, but the murky laws of society declare age to be a communicable disease that requires either boring isolation or the pointless pursuit of death on the golf course, the rich man's route to heaven. The young deprive the Ancients of the responsibility for their lives out of fear and distaste for oldness. They forget they will in turn be so deprived by their own young.

How to avoid the smothering ministrations of your frightened children? How to regain the manly (and womanly) captaincy of your soul? It is really very easy. Remember the lesson of your mother's nipple. Become the world's oldest Boy Scout. Prepare! Prepare!

Prepare for old age with all the passion that you prepared for life. Create an ambience for ancientness that allows the full range of your powers. Pick a field of endeavor that encourages the sobriquet of "sage" rather than "old fart". Store up the wisdom that youth forgets. Become the amazing encyclopedia of a tiny specialty needed only occasionally and thus not a full career for the young. Find yourself a padded niche in which your hoardom achieves sanctity, the whiteness of your beard hints at purity, and a masquerade of decrepitude invites honorable assistance. And never, never, never stop screwing.

A ninety-year-old test pilot may make a wonderful one-time contribution. An ancient linebacker might, with his demise on the field, provide the obligatory stopping of the clock, endowing a much needed moment of rest upon his teammates. Parachute jumping is certainly within the capabilities of the Ancient and the sport can provide a genetically terminal jumper the interesting option of not pulling his ripcord. These are useful suicides, examples of once-only, grand gestures, a last gasp of audacity that costs the gasper very little and saves his children a bundle.

Suicides, however, are not available to Ancients. Our perverse society defines useful suicide as heroism. In war, heroism is a disease of the young and the healthy. Why should not all wars be fought by the Ancients? There would be little additional loss to society, since the combatants are on their way out anyway, and there would be fewer deaths due to the slower and more dignified pace of battle.

The Ancient who wants to remain honored and useful amidst the juvenescent oxen must steal back from them the reins of his existence. He must define his function, not in terms of his strengths, but, in terms of their weaknesses. He must choose, early in his life, fields of endeavor in which, like old wine tasters and art experts, he can go on forever. He must tailor his activity to his physical capabilities (ongoing rather than one-time). He must convince the young that acquired wisdom and an occasional and satisfying tumescence compares favorably to mindless erection.

The effective Ancient will have long since learned that chance is really not chance at all, that risk is mathematics and that most perceived wisdom is a process of the slow release of information to the uninitiated. A cloak of mystery is the very best screen for the shallowness of all human knowledge and our society has already equated mystery with age. Witches are withered, sages are hoary, kings are venerable, Methuselah lived nine hundred years and who but the immortal Mel Brooks could ever conceive of a Young Frankenstein?

Preserve and heighten the mysteries. Narrow the field until the horny young oxen have great trouble squeezing through the gate. Then will you be honored, listened to, fed at the head of the table and beset by maidens intent on testing their beauty and your reluctance. Your more slowly gathering strength will be appreciated as sexual patience and sensitivity, your period of excitation, lengthened by age, will be put to good and adored use by the hitherto hastily unsatisfied maidens and you, you old goat, can saunter down the hill past the frantic oxen and bang 'em all.

There exists one activity so clearly meant for Ancients, so perfectly tailored to their physical capabilities, so cleverly designed to preserve and enhance their vitality that it is bewildering that few, so very few, ever discover it.

It is an activity that has as its prime precondition the slow and unconscious absorption of experience. It is an activity that enlivens the muscles as it oils the joints. It lengthens, preserves and juicifies life. It throws the practitioner among the beautiful and adoring young. It confers an inviolable mantle of authority and allows you to wear a cute hat.

It takes you to faraway places, unreachable by jet by your richer and more moribund contemporaries. It tempts your taste buds with exotic offerings and disallows constipation by scaring the shit out of you. It fills your Ancient eyes with new wonder. It contradicts the cynics and negates the naysayers. It is the way a man, especially an old guy, should live. And perhaps best of all, you may, if you choose (and why not?) use it to wallow luxuriously in the soothing mud hole of the world's envy.

When the alarums and excursions of your life are over, when your kids are doctors and your wives have found better things to do, when your enemies have had their comeuppances and your friends all bore you, when obituaries prove interesting and when the prospect of earning even one more dollar appalls, then the moment has come to look about for a boat in which to sail around the world. There simply ain't nothin' else worth doing.

Long-distance sailing is the perfect antidote for age. Everything on a sailboat is done slowly, thoughtfully and in a rhythm much better suited to the experience of decades than to the inexperience of years. Cruising requires no great expenditure of energy or strength. It is an activity in which hard-acquired skills and subtle bits of information are substituted for the arrogance of young muscle. Old muscle, miserly of its ergs, is perfectly capable of getting all the jobs done that need doing. And when the chips are down and the winds are up and the sea is set on teaching you a lesson, then a young back is no more capable of addressing the sea's immeasurable force than is an old one.

Us old guys are a garrulous lot. We have a lot of miles under our belt, a whole world of experience. We discover, in our senescence, that we know a lot of things. We want to talk about them and to pass them along to the young 'uns. But what greenling wants to be regaled by a grandpapa about his victories on the golf course, or on Seventh Avenue, or how he snared the best seat at the east wall? Yet what sappy progeny, just beginning to sense the wide wonder of the world being offered, will not sit in open-mouthed delight at the tales of derring-do from a lean and leathery ancestor who smells a little funny and wears a cute hat? If nothing else, the cruising life will guarantee a rapt audience forever.

The cardinal difference between an old sailor and a young one is that the old sailor has had the leisure to acquire all the myriad skills necessary for successful cruising. But the process must start early. Time must be stolen from diapers and current events. The questionable delights of the cocktail party must be passed up and the comfort of sleeping in on a rainy Sunday morning must be sacrificed to the need to know how your little boat will act in a squall. The old salts who came before you, all great sailors and all lousy writers, must be read for the lessons they teach. Celestial navigation must be conquered, and like so many of us before you, you must hang out of the bedroom window sighting the moon reflected in a dish of water, endlessly proving and reproving that your house is where you damn well know it is.

And over the years you must beg passages on the boats of more fortunate friends. You must pester them for knowledge and stand your watch and then stand their watch alongside them, lest you miss some sensate sliver of input that will save your life three decades hence. You must be cook, washerup, deck ape and gofer, all in the maniacal pursuit of experience. You must become a royal pain in the ass, but a dependable one who gives back effort and loyalty to compensate for the endless nagging of the skipper for information. You must spend your life preparing so you will have a full life to live when your old life is over.

And when, for the first time, you head your boat out into the open sea, only then will you understand what the preparation was about.

You will be free. Free of the constraints and the tch-tch's of society, free of our imperfect laws, free of the embarrassment and guilt of family and finally free of death. For you have passed through death already in leaving your first life behind. Death can never hold terror for you again.

An old song says it best.

"Good-by to things that bore me,
Life is waiting for me.
I see a new horizon,
My life has only begun,
Beyond the blue horizon
Lies a rising Sun."

BEYOND THE BLUE HORIZON

UNLIKELY PASSAGES

1

Accidental Delights

I joined the Navy
To see the world.
And what did I see?
I saw the Sea.

A Navy Lament

You become a true circumnavigator only when you realize the futility of setting routes and stops. When you abjure these you join that small band who do not know, nor care, where they are going. Take a direction, certainly, but deal cautiously with precision. Hold it away from you between thumb and forefinger and gingerly test its odor. Precision stinks. Open your hand and let it plop softly into the sea. This is your declaration of independence.

The best things that ever happen are the ones you bump into. Accidental successes in business were the only kind that ever delivered me any cheese. My magical women always appeared, magically, out of the fog of my blind imperception. When we learn how little attention the Celestial Spheres pay to our attempts to organize them, we are on the road to contentment.

Setting rigid goals at sea demonstrably is a feckless pursuit. The sea has taught me (almost too late) that life on land is plagued by unreachable goals and ennervating expectations. So much energy is devoured in pushing rivers that can be so much more comfortably navigated floating downstream.

Sailboats almost never go *to* anyplace, no matter how hard you try. They go *toward* someplace and take, en route, what the winds and the tides have to offer. On my circumnavigation I started from Miami headed towards the Caymans. But in the Yucatan Channel we banged up against a wind blowing in a perverse direction. The resulting seas were terrifying and the only possible course was Cozumel, a lovely island where we spent a week in a small garden restaurant eating the best Italian food I had ever tasted.

Another time I tried to get away from Sri Lanka at the wrong time of year. After six days of beating our brains out to the southwest we gave up and sailed northeast to India, where I fell in love and learned more about myself than I thought possible.

Departing the Canaries heading westward towards Barbados some 3,000 miles downwind, we ended up in Dakar, hundreds of miles to the east on the coast of Africa. I would not have missed my year there nor would I have made it, except by accident. At the end of each misdirection lay adventure and delight. A larger power was offering me, over and over, a world that I was purposefully planning to avoid.

The wonderful absence of precision is the great attraction of cruising. You have had a bellyfull of boarding the 8:42 in Huntington and getting off at Penn Station at 9:31. Day after day the expected continued until in your secret heart you yearned for a little train wreck. (God willing no one should get killed.) Anything to confound the constancy. Anything to disrupt the dulling routine that stretches out to your last days.

With a sailboat you buy the means to seek out change and adventure, to set yourself free. But always remember the very nature of the cruising life disallows even well-laid plans. At sea such plans lie beyond the mathematics of probability. Plans are for the landbound.

If you have places you yearn for and are set on going to, remember the sea has its own plans for you. Everything about sailing the big oceans conspires to change touring plans, not the least of which are your own discoveries of ports you cannot leave: a new lover, a spectacular piece of mountain, a field by the sea calling out for a plow, or perhaps the touch of an irresistible mind. Each may separately, or all together, leave you surprised and gasping on the beach.

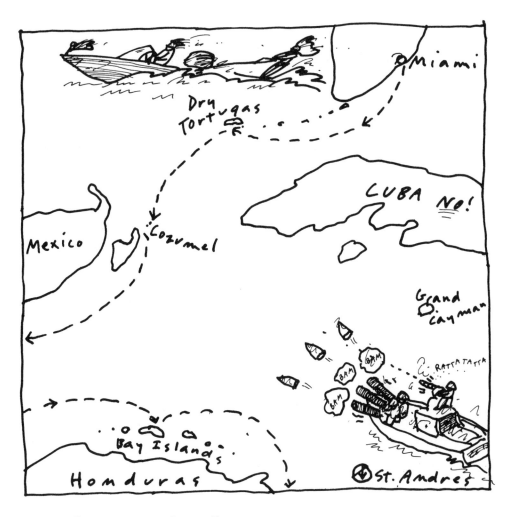

Sailing Directions I

The Portugese navigators of the 15th century started keeping logs of their voyages of discovery into oceans unknown to Western mariners. These logs held what were then the world's most sacred and inviolable secrets. For almost a century Portugese skippers were able to reserve for themselves the benefits of these valuable compendia of sailing information, which later became the Sailing Directions, *now published by various governments (ours being one). They make*

5

the most marvelous reading. They are filled with detailed and arcane information, little line sketches of landfalls and lighthouses and mountains. They give depths and warnings of hazards and port requirements and anything else a skipper entering a port for the first time will be curious about.

Buy the Sailing Directions *and buy another fascinating book,* Ocean Passages for the World *and between the two armchair your way around the world. Through the magic of mind and your own only half-understood needs, your chair will transform into a sound hull and billowing sails and you will be on your way.*

To give you an assist I detail below and throughout the book my own passages around the globe. I started from Miami, where fitting out is made easy by a hundred good marine sources and where the weather allows a departure anytime of the year. The first legs from Miami are short island hops to the west through some of the loveliest cruising waters in the world. You could start from Topeka, but why bother?

Sail southward from Miami. Curve around the Keys. Lie overnight off the Dry Tortugas. After the powerboats have scurried away, the last two hundred years disappear. Then sail southwest. Avoid Cuba where they will not let you land even in a fierce gale. Visit Cozumel and then cruise south along whatever of the west coast of Central America is still open to us Gringos. Do not miss the Bay Islands off the east coast of Honduras and buy lots of half-buck-a-pound coffee. Coffee makes a wonderful insulator. You can even line your fridge with it. Be very careful of St. Andres Island. The military is in fear of invasion and is likely to mistake your 40-foot sailboat for an enemy battlecruiser. They will shoot first and then they will clean their glasses.

2

Love and Sex On A Sailboat

If you are sailing around the world on a small boat it is
necessary for you to deal with love and sex in a new context
—one that is both discordant and perverse.

Rules defining sexual and emotional needs are altered at
sea. Nothing in sex and love feels exactly correct anymore,
and all of your careful practice and hard-won facility with
that other sex just doesn't seem to parse. (If indeed it ever
did.)

Since women are demonstrably a separate species from
men, they respond to the alteration of sex at sea differently
than men do. Thus whatever observations a sailorman might
make will have to be made, in the obverse, by a sailorwoman.
Our bodies may be profiled to exactly fit, but our geists do
not. It is this mismatch (God's small oversight) that we dis-
cuss here.

Sex is a terrifying business to most of us. It takes us a long
time to come to terms with what is essentially a simple process. Some of us—most perhaps—never do reach accommodation, and live out our lives behind a veil of sexual
desperation. At sea this coupling becomes distorted beyond

recognition. Even the most successful practitioners must all attempt a new accommodation in a world of sexual twilight. Since not many of us completed the first go-round with any style, this second run at the target is no less confusing.

On a sailboat, relations between women and men can be both the best of times and the worst of times. There are moments of great freedom and exhilaration and then, in a nanosecond, moments of grinding constraint.

There is no middle ground on a small boat, no neutral corner to catch your breath and recoup. You either are enormously successful or an abject failure. It's not too different from what happens on land except that at sea there is no blessed release of separation. Your partner cannot escape your failures and, what might be worse, you cannot escape your imagined victories. A small boat is the ultimate killing ground. It tests the sailor as a human being in the most vulnerable aspect of his humanity, in the intricate mysteries of sex.

At sea everything sexual is parable and paradox, even the accidents of initial choice. It is both simple and difficult for a sailor to commence a sexual liaison. The shifting of bed partners between boats is oiled by the obvious unity of interests, and encouraged by the fact that relationships between cruising sailors do not often have the restrictions of custom and family. On the other hand, finding a new partner is difficult because the population from which a choice is made is extremely small. Sailorwomen have always been a rare breed. Beset as they are by biological directives and societal no-no's, there still are far fewer sailorwomen out there than there are counterparts. However, despite the difficulties sailors do manage more dalliance than most.

But occasional bedding is entirely peripheral (however attractive it may be) to the real needs of the sailor. A sailorman needs a mate who is more than a wife or mistress or sometime liaison—more than a helper, crew or cook. The male sailor needs all the other sides of his own inadequacies manifested in one woman. He needs to realize in his mate his unacknowledged dreams and desires.

A woman who enters into a passage with a man must be too many things. She must be physically strong to haul line and anchor (penile chauvinism still insists on the prerogative of the helm on entering harbor), she must be calm and responsive in danger and emergencies, she must be a magician in the galley and a shrew in the marketplace, she must be a doctor, nurse and Mommy. And let it also be noted that she must be (in his eyes) both desirable and beautiful. Beyond all other prescription, she must be capable of high and exalted eroticism, since sex on a sailboat can be a terrible mess and sometimes even painful.

Just as the sailorwoman must drift beyond female for her man, he also must transcend his maleness. A melding, rather than a joining, is needed. That delightful and fulfilling game of sex role reversal can be successfully and unselfconsciously played out in your forty feet of sailing universe. Nowhere else is this game of switched labors and emotions so desperately unnecessary. Unless work and tasks and attitudes are fully interchangeable, there is little possibility of a melding. Attempting to maintain traditional sexual tensions while necessarily sharing equally the responsibilities and the labors of keeping a small boat safe simply does not work. Sexual tensions are a product of socially designed inequality and on land are not subject to resolution. At sea the tensions are resolved and put aside in the comforting twilight of sexual equality. At sea the hard glare of unresolved sexual tensions causes expectations to shrivel. Adventure becomes mere travelogue.

On land, with all the varied input of personality and all of the soothing generosity of space, the man/woman thing becomes a discontinuous series of close encounters, sensibly interspersed with healing periods of discontinuity. On land we are blessed with a little relief from one another, distancing where faults can be aligned into perspective and where passion can be rekindled by absence.

Not so on an extended passage in a small vessel. There is no distance, no time apart and no relief. Everything must be dealt with in the immediate now. On the land a series of tangential connections between otherwise warring parties becomes at sea an absolute and unbroken skinscape with all hairy warts revealed. George Bernard Shaw once said that marriage was an attractive institution because it combined the maximum of temptation with the maximum of availability. How naive and Victorian. Availability shrivels temptation. Closeness denies passion. Too much opportunity oppresses. The Dance of the Seven Veils must be raised exponentially, eroticism must reach stratospheric heights to overcome the constant and irritating view of the warts.

A small boat brings out physical ugliness in us. Awkward squatting and stretching is the rule. Clumsiness is taught to our bodies by the motion of the boat. Nausea is not nice, and we are forced to share smells and sounds in total, ceaseless intimacy.

The toilet has a thin door (or none) and the lack of fresh air is endemic, so you must live with, and love, the smell of her relief. There is simply no room on a sailboat for the pedestal on which so much of the real in woman is hidden. Her clay feet are dirty and calloused, her nails are torn by her sailorly labors and her hair is stringy from the lack of fresh water. It is all there, without surcease, in front of you . . . her smells, her juices and each month her very blood.

And so is yours, my male friend, so is yours. It is not a one-way street. Men abuse eye, nose and psyche as well. The blood may not be so regular but the pimples are larger and, while the moon does not titrate men's emotions as forcefully, we are not immune to its lunacy. Because men are so much more closed and fragile to begin with, the impact of closeness on the male is even more telling. A thoughtless glance at our waistline or a lighthearted and friendly observation about last night's romp can, like a collision at sea, ruin our entire day.

If love is to survive it must become transcendent. It must be able to rise above imperfections glossed over on land. Constipation must be considered, diarrhea debated and urinary tract infections shared (which they usually are anyway).

On land successful sex is distilled of desire denied by absence, of comfort and warmth, of cleanliness, good smells and the languor of plenty of time. Sex requires seduction, the odd surprise of a chilled bottle of good wine, and an occasional single red rose. At best coitus is chancy, orgasm not guaranteed and when, as it often is, unsuccessful, it requires some distancing and the licking of wounds in private.

Nothing remotely resembles these idyllic conditions on a small boat on a long passage. If you had to describe the least best ambience for good, healthy and satisfying screwing, it would be a little vessel, either lurching about in an unruly sea or wallowing sickeningly in a glassy calm. Under these conditions desire is dulled by endless presence, comfort is only dimly remembered, excess heat (or cold) is debilitating, cleanliness is impossible, and the smells are anything but appealing. The languor of time is rare. Customs officers took your last bottle of wine and seduction is just too damn much trouble.

How in the world can two people ever get it on, let alone keep getting it on, under such unfelicitous circumstances? Clearly it is an impossibility.

Nevertheless, it can be done. It has been done. Great love affairs do blossom and grow on world passages. There is no formula for a successful love affair at sea, even less than for one on land.

If you are going sailing and want to experience the full impact of the adventure, you must raise the passionate commitment to your lover to a very high power. Just as you must totally defer to your boat and her needs, you must single-mindedly enter into a constant, observant and loving pas de deux with your mate.

On land this impaction of sexual egos, one into the other, is made almost impossible by the soaring volume of input from surrounding events. But at sea the only events are those generated by the two of you. There is no one else. It is as if the only people left in the world are you and she, so you two had damn well better make it work. For all you know the survival of the human race depends on it.

The very factor that most destroys great love affairs on land, endless intimacy, can be the binding thong that makes love work at sea. People, planet, universe and God are encompassed by just two lovers floating about in an intimacy from which, by lack of comparison, all pejoration has been removed. You have been granted a new beginning and there are no apple trees on board.

Beyond the emotional lies that little devil, screwing. Who of us has not had the wild impulse to giggle at a skin flick? On the best of beds, on the most solid of foundations, the rigors and the acrobatics of coitus are daunting.

There is a school of sex which, in its reach for ever more bizarre and impossible excitements, seeks ever more bizarre and impossible coital positions. The more impossible the physical interlock, the more satisfaction is generated. To these creative folk I extend an invitation to a bedding on a small boat. Here the most bizarre positions are achieved, not openly because of the absolute stricture of available space ("Now where the hell are we going to put that leg?"), but also in response to the endless sway and lurch, and the belly-sinking drops, of a sailboat. In any sort of sea an entirely new calculus of coitus is created. Nowhere can more variety be achieved than with the sea composing an infinitely random catalog of comings together.

And of comings apart. The slightest moment of inattention and one of you may be cast fully to starboard while the other remains emptily to port. If, as is usually the case, the flingee is flung downward to lee, then the return to paradise becomes an exhausting uphill climb accompanied by a growing disinclination to continue the acceptance of abuse.

During any act of intercourse a great deal of holding on takes place. Holding on to your partner, to your orgasm, to your sanity, to your control and to your sense of humor. At sea you also are unreasonably required to hold on to the boat, least when you zig it should zag, resulting in either mashed members, or in total disengagement with your flag waving helplessly in the air. Intercourse on a small sailboat is a major adventure even if you never leave port. If you do, fasten your seatbelts.

Having said all this, and having turned some off sailing and some off sex, be assured there are high and irreplaceable moments that, with luck, stretch into a lifetime. A bed of fluffy foresail on deck, the exquisitely erotic impact of a sunset at sea, the indescribable welcome of a warm and dry body after four hours of abuse by rain and cold and, finally, the total peace of coming into port after the alarms and challenges of the sea—all are the sailor's reward.

All is contrast. The soft and protective warmth of your lover's body is the other side of the cold coin of terror of the sea. Nowhere can sex and love be more satisfying and more worthwhile to achieve than here, alone, at sea in your own private universe.

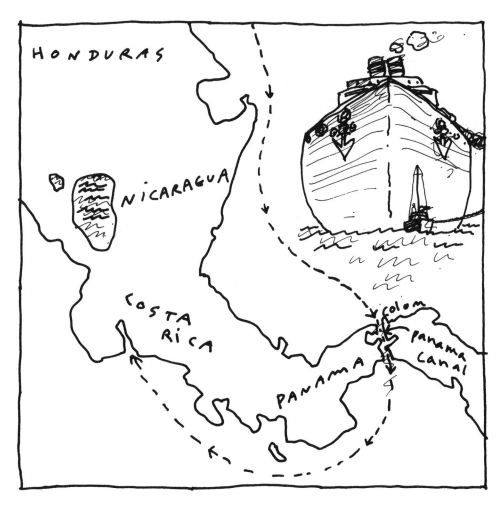

Sailing Directions II

From St. Andres Island sail south and transit the Panama Canal. Despite canard the Panamanian officials are polite and efficient. The folks in Panama are less anti-American than I would expect after having been occupied by the U.S. for so long. However, do avoid Colon on the eastern end. It is desperately poor and if you wander about that city you likely will be relieved of watch, wallet and a pint of blood.

The actual transit of the Canal is a gas. It takes a full day

—sunrise to sunset—and you will be accompanied by a knowledgeable Panamanian pilot. Their acceptance of you is skin deep at best. Do not try throwing any weight around, remember it is their country now. To transit, you need four lengths of dock line, each 200 feet long. These will be handled by the longshoremen in a sailorly fashion as they juggle you into the ponderous locks. The screws of the tanker transiting with you are bigger than your boat. So be very careful and try not to be creative. Do exactly what you are told.

The Cuts through the high hills are engineering triumphs and pieces of history. If you squint your eyes and let your mind drift you almost can see the hordes of pig-tailed Chinese at work and the great "engines" that were built to separate the continents. If you are not excited in anticipation of the Canal, you will be afterwards.

Next, wander north for a bit to Costa Rica where you will find shoals of sailors washed up on shore and disinclined to leave this lovely country. Look for an ancient, bearded American sailor with one leg who also will not leave. He has a restaurant and, while a bit crusty, he is wonderfully helpful and irreverent.

3

Trivia

Upon trivia are noble passages built. On trivia are all sailing voyages founded, and founder. Social twinges that on land would be unworthy of the merest note, become overwhelmingly important at sea.

Everything on a small boat aggravates more, itches more and outrages more. Who would care on land if your companion at the dinner table is left handed? At sea this simple matter can be the source of a major conflagration of wills, since a quick exchange of places in a dining room becomes an exhausting dance at sea. And a bit of flatulence? Unpleasant in your bedroom, but a cause for undying hatred in the close confines of the fo'c'sle.

When measured against the ebullient canvas of a Pacific sunset, these are small matters indeed. But these small matters must be addressed or you will never get to see that sunset. There is so much agony in the closeness of a sailboat it is a wonder that anyone sails other than singlehanded. But we are a gregarious breed and thus the need to share great events and beautiful moments comes in direct conflict with the corrosiveness of contiguity.

On one memorable passage I was taught the immense power of trivial events, and how easily we are detoured from our heart's delights by non-consequential matters. Of the three corporal delights of passage, eating, sleeping, and dalliance, only sleeping was available to the skipper. No one wanted to cook and dalliance was denied because I was unmated; a condition I have been at pains not to repeat. The fog of Democracy had descended upon my little kingdom, followed immediately by the wild winds of anarchy. Everyone was doing what pleased each most and the devil take the skipper and his appetites.

I toyed briefly with the impulse to exercise my authority and order up, in a loud and captainlike tone, my dinner. But experience has taught that the giver of unacceptable orders on a small boat pays the piper. A crew has so many pathological pathways of retaliation, that the dangerous game of imperiously shouted orders is never worth the candle.

With women crew it is a doubly dangerous gambit. What skipper can resist the hurt little looks and the tears with which women have dominated us since they preceded us out of the slime? I also suspect that there exists an international network of vaginal telegraphy that would spread my name among the distaff legions as a male undeserving of the favors of dalliance. Lysistrata lives!

Discretion being the better part of valor and the major part of cowardice, I decided to hunker down and await developments. They came quickly.

Our medical doctor decided he only wanted to do doctoring, although we were a remarkably healthy group. One of the women, a philosophy major, wanted only to ponder and the other, a psychiatrist, spent a good deal of time practicing on her couch. Finally my last remaining winch grinder, a geologist, declared it his duty to observe and note any rocks that might float by.

This was too much. The skipper had to act. So, standing

arms akimbo and something less than rock-solid on the lurching deck, I cried, "All will cook, all will wash up and all will stand watch!"

This leaden balloon sank into the bilge and took with it any hope of a friendly passage. Clouds of discontent gathered on the horizon. Squall lines formed and lightning bolts accumulated voltage. The tension became palpable. Rebellion and mutiny flashed through my mind. Suddenly I pictured myself in an open boat with only a cask of water.

As is usually the case, it was one of the less egomaniacal sex who did the Gordian bit by offering to do all the cooking and all the washing in exchange for being excused from standing watch. This felicitous suggestion was applauded by all and the skipper graciously agreed, with mounting hunger.

I was doubly delighted since I knew that, other than the volunteer, no one could cook. The last of my shredded authority was preserved and my gut was reprieved from a crew who could not find a hot stove in a small galley with both hands. The meals would have been dreadful.

This calls to mind a tale about a group camping out in the wilds who agreed that each would take a turn at the campfire until someone complained. Then it would become the complainer's turn to cook.

Cooker number one set out to produce meals of such insult to tongue and palate that, in a civilized setting, would have caused his instant demise. He was fishing for insults but caught only glowers.

In desperation he went into the woods and gathered bear droppings. He cooked, seasoned and simmered them and awaited the inevitable complaints, any one of which would free him from servitude. Gasps of incredulity came. Retching was heard as was gagging, but no complaint. Finally one poor soul reared back and gasped,

"Tastes like shit!" then quickly, "But it's delicious."

We sailors must deal with the trivia. We must arrange our

perceptions so the smallest irritation does not destroy the largest adventure. Some have already conquered their devils. But they are in the clear minority. The rest of us are too busy endlessly and forever proving ourselves right at the expense of our companions. An argument over whose socks belong in what drawer quickly segues away from socks and into the arid battleground of will. Is it my will or his that emerges triumphant? Memories deep in our prehistoric, reptilian brain remind us that the victor eats the vanquished. We never are far from the slime.

Our brains will do anything to survive: lie, cheat, steal and even play dead to live to die another day. Any battle, once joined by the brain—even over the tiniest complaint—must then be fought out in the largest context, that of survival itself. We are the repository of the many brains of our evolutionary climb. We do not rid ourselves of old brains, we just add to them and cover them up. But they remain vital and with their autonomic passions intact, lay in wait for affronts.

It is our smallest, most primitive brain, our reptilian, that is the biggest culprit. It knows only eat or be eaten. It cannot differentiate between a slight and a deadly threat. All is deadly threat and all affront is met with total war. It does not know how to negotiate. This reptilian remnant knows only the threat of extinction.

On a small boat, the endless taunting of the reptile in us allows the trivial to become cosmic. Good friends walk coldly away from each other after a few weeks at sea.

And yet there are great passages and great sailing companions. Perhaps the great passages happen when each of us withdraws into the vast spaces of self, when each chooses not to interact on any but the most needful levels. We do not go to sea to achieve a "meaningful relationship" with others, but for exactly the opposite reason, to achieve relationship with self.

This must be why, after a good passage, you cannot remember very much of what happened and after a bad one you cannot forget.

Trivia is the devil that ruins passages, marriages, lives and even international affairs. A nuclear holocaust, if it ever happens, will not result from a philosophic decision to end the world. It will happen when some tiny squirt of the hormone of outrage links up, for the briefest moment (all that is necessary), with the concept of push the button.

The solution in all cases is to remove the friction, to banish the trivia.

One axiom of the Philosophy of Trivia is that there is no corrosive trivia inside your own head. Everything in there deserves and gets, equal consideration. It is only when—in passages, marriages, lives and nuclear confronts—when your head must deal with another's head, that the imperfect and unequal perception of what is trivial leads, ultimately, to holocaust. Be it small or large it is holocaust just the same.

What is needed is space. Space in which to avoid another's perception of importance. Space to swing your spiritual cat without impinging on someone else's emotional dog. And that is impossible on a small sailboat unless you recognize there can be no companionship at sea. Precious little on land, if you want to get along, but none, absolutely none, at sea.

Find the solution you claim to seek. Push your shipmates away from you. Sleep rather than talk, read rather than relate and train yourself to see and hear nothing save the infinite delight and excitement of which self is capable.

And if you do . . . and if you can . . . just watch the approval grow in the eyes of your mates, so that, after impolitely ignoring them for all of the time you were together, you will hear them sing your praises as a great sailing comrade.

And you, in lovely and loving paradox, will think the same of them.

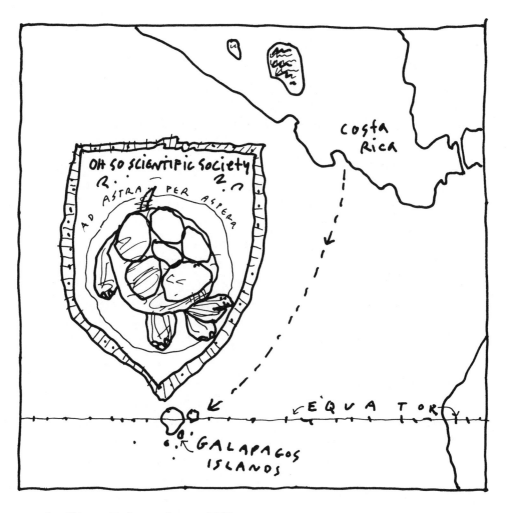

Sailing Directions III

Less than a thousand miles to the southwest of Costa Rica lies the magic Archipelago of Galapagos. Writing about the Galapagos Islands is a useless pursuit. The Galapagos are felt in the belly, not experienced in the head.

The very best hotel in the world is on the main island. It is the Hotel Galapagos (sounds slightly funny to me) and until recently was run by an American who had been in the Islands since before the Beagle. It is long and rambling and usually empty but features the most exciting guest book I have ever seen. Every great name, and most of the near-great, have passed through here and signed with extravagant praise. Sign off your boat for a week and let the mystery of the islands percolate up through your feet. Do it at the Hotel Galapagos. My memories are of great music in the common room, Grand Marnier, Gila monsters and a personal rite of passage best kept deliciously in the mind.

The proprietor, now dead, was a leathery Ancient. He had come early to the Galapagos and had the good sense to stay. Every few years he would take a nubile native girl to his bed and, upon putting her aside for a nubiler one, it was his style to set each up in a little business of her own.

The Galapagos are hard to get into. Private yachts are forbidden but these islands are not to be missed for lack of creativity. There is a way. Listen closely. Invent a fictitious oceanographic research institute. Print stationery on which you are identified as the research director. Create, from whole cloth, a board of directors of international names just slightly malapropped (Elliot Roosenvelt, Jak Coosteaux and, what the hell, Winston Churchbell). Fire off a request to Ecuador that your "research" vessel be permitted to visit the Darwin Institute in the Galapagos for information not available elsewhere.

Give it a shot. If it doesn't work, sail in under medical protest—drink a glass of Galapagosian water, the worst in the world by scientific test. If you do not die, you get to stay. If you do die, there is no better place to wrap it up than in those theurgic isles, which are closer to God than anyplace else on Earth.

Let My People Sail

Lord knows I am no moralist and Lord knows I don't believe in Him, but I do believe in the elegant purity of some of Someone's inventions. I believe in man, I believe in His spirit in man and I firmly believe that all hypocrites will either burn in Hell or be forever bored to distraction in Heaven.

On land, it is not possible to conform to the Ten Commandments. I have no problem with my landlubberly friends who choose to covet their neighbor's ass or indeed their neighbor's wife's ass. I do not object to their disbelief in God, or their failing to honor the Sabbath or stealing or lying. They are excused from the Commandments because our society is one for which the Commandments were never designed.

The tribal glue that stuck our lives and the Commandments together is gone. God is either dead or very ill and the only sin left is hypocrisy. On land our naked selves are hidden and our natures are subjected to ethics that bend and wave in the winds of convenience. The situational ethics we live by are no longer tied to our survival. We can say one thing and do another with impunity. We cannot be found out. Life on land is too turgid and turgidity is the petri dish of the hypocrite.

At sea we cannot avoid being found out. We sailors have no better natures than our brothers on land, but we lack the space and the opportunity to lie, cheat and steal. Concealment of the truth about ourselves is uncomfortably impossible. We have only one situation. We are constrained by circumstances to live by an ethical standard designed for that one situation. We are hoist on our own petard.

Life at sea is only an analog of life on land. It is a simplified model from which has been abstracted the confusing background radiation of society and most of the opportunities for deceit. What is left is the essence of being alive close alongside other people, each of whom has come to know what is in the others' hearts. We cannot dissemble for lack of a place to hide. We are a small group of passionate people sharing only one common experience and sharing and knowing the good and the bad about each other. Thus is a sailboat's crew a tribe.

The Ten Commandments were tailored for just such a group of zealots, living in a tight tribal community in which everything each member did was visible and understood by his neighbor. With this in mind the Ten Commandments, while incompetent on land, become blindingly apropos for a sailing passage.

A sailboat on a long passage creates the archetypical tribal conditions of unfettered, unlimited and undressed closeness. At sea the Ten Commandments work. At sea abrasive closeness is oiled and made possible by the clarity of rules of conduct. If the tribe is to survive, and if the vessel is to make port, then a set of rules must be agreed upon.

The Word of God is curiously difficult to improve upon and writing better rules than His for the eleventh tribe (the sailing tribe) would be a dangerous act. Better to use His, especially since the moment will surely come—I guarantee it—when even the agnostic sailor, faced with unacceptable odds, will seek His intercession.

I Am the Lord Thy God.

At sea it is an emotional and intellectual impossibility for most of us not to believe. There are, possibly, a few sailors who are able to accept the idea of undirected natural malevolence, but I am not one of them. A fierce wind and forty-foot seas cannot be dealt with absent the final refuge of belief in something. This Commandment directs us to believe—very easy for a sailor.

Make No Idols or False Gods

If you are dealing with a hurricane, making a God out of it is less than satisfying. Why pray to the very thing that is trying to destroy you? What you need is a transcendent concept that lets you understand your place and the hurricane's place in a grander scheme.

Calling on The Name of The Lord in Vain

Listen, if you are dumb enough to be out there in a Clorox bottle, praying for intercession just won't work. If I were God and I heard a desperate plea from some asshole who challenged My oceans in an ill-conceived cockleshell, I think I would be inclined to ignore him. The meaning of this Commandment is, call upon neither God nor the Coast Guard for help to which you are not entitled.

Remember the Sabbath

Since He is a reasonable (He had better be, since He invented reason) being, I am sure some stretching of this Commandment is allowed. When Moses lay on his deathbed, the people asked for his final advice. Moses said, "Choose Life." The Lord, knowing that his children must work to survive on a sailboat, always will allow us to choose life. I could never believe in a being who, having invented life, would ask us to deny it on one day out of each seven.

We have a special way of dealing with the Sabbath on my boat. Each crew member, in rotation, is awarded a seventh day. He or she may then define the personal nature of his Sabbath. One might choose to heave-to on Sabbath eve and spend a quiet, workless 24 hours. Another might choose to ease the sheets from a beat to the tranquility of a reach and consider that rest enough. When it is her Sabbath, another of my crew always says, "Sail on—but in silence." Enforced silence for a whole day aboard a small sailboat is the highest form of honoring the Sabbath and it saves your sanity.

But when you are really in trouble, when the wind is beyond hearing and the seas beyond sense, He has already prepared for you a workable method of obeying His Commandment. The very best way to deal with an ultimate storm is to lie ahull. Take down all sail, tie your rudder amidships and commit yourself to His grace. Then you can go below and light candles or get drunk. Both are allowed.

Honor Your Father and Your Mother

Since you were shaped by your parents you are living out their unconscious directives whether or not they acknowledge it. You would not be out there, in harm's way, had they not some driving passion for freedom. You honor them in each of your passages much more than you ever could by becoming president of the Men's Club.

You Shall Not Commit Murder

OK, and anyway it would leave you shorthanded. Nowhere is the simple fact of interdependence and the precious value of every being more clear than at sea.

You Shall Not Commit Adultery

On a thirty-foot sailboat? Are you kidding?

You Shall Not Steal

Nothing anyone owns on a sailboat means anything unless it can be used and shared by all. Why steal? It's all there to borrow, anyway. And if some idiot does steal something, where does he get to enjoy it? The tribal intimacy of a small sailboat guarantees the foolishness of theft.

You Shall Not Lie About Your Neighbor

If there is to be any pleasure, or any success or even survival on a long sailing passage, there must be absolute honesty. If you start to protect your ass by lying about the others aboard, the passage will be destroyed. You will be found out, anyway. On land, endless ways exist to murder truth. On a sailboat the truth has you by the throat. It is inescapable. Everybody knows everything about each other on a boat (a good definition of a tribe) so a lie becomes as unacceptable as a hard suitcase. Liars are either quickly cured or quickly signed off.

You Shall Not Covet Your Neighbor's Wife,
Servant, Ox or Ass

Listen, the only things worth coveting on a long passage are the sea, the stars, the glory of the sunset, good companions and the special delight of shared experience. He didn't say a damned thing about not coveting these—so go ahead. And anyway, if you should get a bit out of line and get to coveting more than you can chew, He can always send a thunderbolt or, in a gentler mood, a rainbow as a reminder of His Covenant with you.

Lord knows I am no moralist and Lord knows I don't believe in Him but sometimes it is very hard not to.

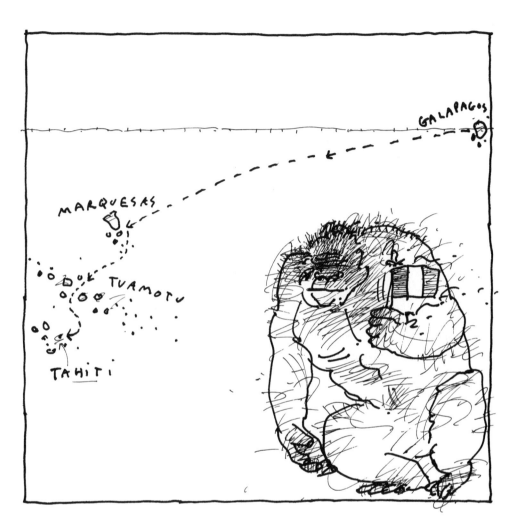

Sailing Directions IV

From the Galapagos sail toward the setting sun, wherein lies Tahiti. Just before you get there give yourself a treat and jog north to the Marquesas. Tahiti without tourists, wild, empty and geography like where King Kong lived. You may be discouraged from staying very long in this paradise by an invention of nature second only to mosquitoes: French colonial officials.

From the Marquesas sail south down through the Tua-

33

motus, invisible in their flatness and dangerous. The squalls are fierce and the water too shallow for comfort. The entrances to these enchanting atolls are hard to find and unmarked. Take your time and do it. They usually are unvisited. Live coral reefs are scattered like pockmarks on the moon. Then sail on to Tahiti, with the highest prices in the world and the uncomfortable smell of French colonialism. Too bad about the jetport but still enough left of l'ancien regime to make it worthwhile. The food is breathtaking and the flowers perfume a thousand square miles of sea.

There is something peculiarly correct about being in Tahiti. It has always been the circumnavigator's goal. On your arrival you join the very special club of those who sailed there. You may do a dozen transatlantics, but not until you have made your landfall in Tahiti will anyone but your mother consider you a bona fide blue-water skipper.

5

Terror and Promise

The moment in my life of purest terror and purest exaltation occurred the first time I put my stern to land and headed my bow out towards a speck of island a thousand miles away. I was Hajii on Jihad. I felt that special exultation that a sanctified Moslem warrior must experience as he joins in his Holy War, as he seeks his death in battle to guarantee his passage to Paradise. My Jihad was a joining of death, the most terror-ridden human emotion, with the most uplifting, the promise of eternal life.

I set my compass irrevocably on ninety degrees. It was a definitive moment, not subject to consideration or reservation. It was my Holy War and I could not lose. Either I would find Paradise in death or Paradise in life. Given my druthers, I, like Moses, would choose life. My feelings in that transcendent moment alternated between my rational fear of the unknown and my overweening, passionate, irrational need to be there. Terror and promise were irresistible.

My fear was anesthetized by ignorance. Full of fear as I was, I was unable to picture what I was afraid of. That made the departure possible. I had generalized fears typical of all sailors—fire at sea, collision, sinking, hurricane or just being lost. But the specifics of drowning or burning were as dim to me as is to the Moslem warrior the possibility of a bullet in the throat and the choking death it brings.

Despite this ignorance, my fear was palpable. It reached into my chest with its ghostly hand. I felt its coldness lying in my body. It crouched there like a cancer, conquerable only by the accumulation of feet, then yards, then miles of wake. I was to defeat my terror, but only a thousand miles further on, when I was to find in the deep oceans my heart's desire.

There was, however, no way for me not to be there. There was no mechanism in my confused and confusing soul with power enough to oppose the crushing need I had to place my boat and my innocent crew in harm's way. It was ordained, predestined. It was my Karma and all this from the most dedicated of rational Western ideologues.

Well, man's life on Earth is nothing if not paradox, and there I sat at the tiller of a blessedly tough thirty-two-foot sailboat, urged on into I could not imagine what, by God, Karma or my equally inscrutable hormones. I was out of control. Deliciously, deleriously, dangerously abandoning myself to elemental forces. It was a high religious experience. I wanted to join with the elemental, wanted to touch on forces unthinkably beyond my own powers and perceptions. If I had been orthodoxly religious, I would have been in church. But I was not and I was therefore at sea. I knew God did not live in the carefully dressed Apostolic stones of man. He was in the elemental sea, and so was I.

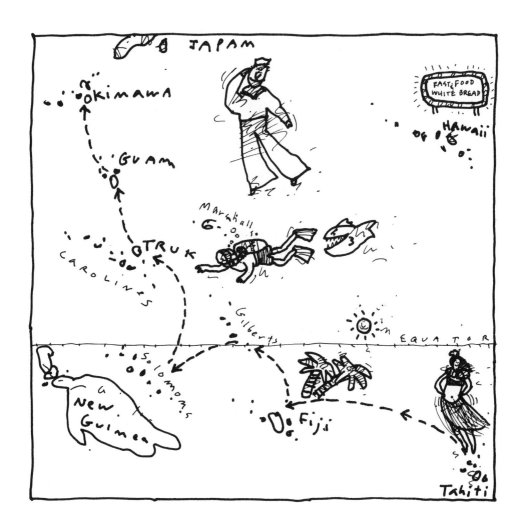

Sailing Directions V

To the northwest from Tahiti you can choose from among the thousands of islands of Fiji and Gilbert and Solomon and Caroline. (Hawaii is a bit to windward and too much like Pittsburgh.) Do not miss Truk, especially if you are a scuba typer. The diving there among the WWII wrecks is worth the trip. Continue to climb up through the islands, each never more than a daysail apart. How long you stay and which you choose to stay at is a choice from among an embarrassment of riches.

Continue northwest towards Guam and Okinawa. Both have kept the flavor of General of the Armies MacArthur. Guam remains an American island and Okinawa just recently was returned to the Japanese. Both are ripe with ice cream, American cars and nice-looking guys with short haircuts. The military is in charge and should you be in any kind of mechanical funk after your own TransPac, the services will fix you up. It is a good idea to seek out the military in any port you happen to be in. They are wonderful and you are welcomed not only as an American but as one of their own, as the adventurer they all see themselves to be.

HydroPhobias

We are anesthetized against most terrors of land. We are so used to them that the most fearful of events get only passing notice from us. There is no more perilous activity in creation than crossing a street trafficked by two-ton iron behemoths, powered by hundreds of horses and guided by a pin-head incapable of finding his backside with a road map. Yet we do it every day. And our kids do it and the mothers of our fathers (being less agile, at somewhat higher risk) do it.

Our fear of this terrifying scenario has been lost in familiar repetition. We have done it ninety-nine times so can the hundredth be so bad? The hundredth is no less dangerous, it simply is not perceived with fear. The terror has been torn out, leaving only the unconcerned living and the uncaring dead.

The fear of pain is a far better convincer than pain itself. HydroPhobias begin on land long before casting off. But once at sea, fear quickly is lost in the joys and the pleasures of the passage. During life-threatening emergencies at sea, fear is drowned in adrenalin—it doesn't have a chance. Out there, you forget to be afraid.

The sea takes no umbrage at anyone's lack of fear. But show one brief flash of disrespect and she will either destroy you or give you a savage knocking about. Like most women, the sea abhors being taken for granted. Ignore her at your mortal peril.

At sea, unlike crossing busy streets, very little repetition is necessary to excise fear. One big storm, one long passage, one toothache, one close encounter with a black freighter or one trepidous trip through pirate waters is vaccine enough for a lifetime. If he can survive it once, the sailor reasons, he can survive it twice. Just knowing what the sea will do to him is armor enough.

There are three HydroPhobias. The Big Three. Two of the Big Three are fears that prevent landlubbers from becoming sailors. The third is primal and common to all mankind. The Big Three are 1) Fear of Flatland, 2) Fear of Being with Self, and 3) The Fear of Bogeymen.

The non-sailor's first and overriding fear is Fear of Flatland, the fear of becoming lost at sea and falling off the edge of the world. The sea conjures up a maze filled with dead ends that constantly turn the boat toward the fearsome lip. Reasonable argument can not persuade the Flatland dwellers that not only is it unlikely you will get lost, it is patently impossible not to find a safe port.

Timid sailors who know the world is round but still fear being lost cling tightly to the shores of the great oceans. Not only are they timid but, ironically, it is near shore that the sea's danger is greatest. You can bop around in a good sailboat in the middle of an ocean for months and never once be even close to mortal peril. There is just nothing out there for you to run into. But every single second you are on soundings you live with the threat of losing your vessel. The best advice when a storm comes up or when you are not exactly sure of where you are is: run for the deeps. In the deeps lies safety. Fear of Deeps keeps the fainthearted sailor in deep jeopardy.

The sea, unbeknownst to those uninitiated to the true nature of navigation, is cluttered with signposts. If by chance the signs are a bit unclear, why just sail on. They soon will decrypt. And if they should not, then sail on. Every ocean is bounded by land somewhere. The day that it was convincingly demonstrated that the earth is, indeed, round and that no boat ever will fall off an edge into a bottomless pit, was the day that all fear of being lost at sea should have evaporated. The problem is these phobics *know* the earth is flat.

Close behind this fear of helplessly dropping off is the Fear of Being with Self, also called the Fear of Boredom. "What do you do with yourself all that time? Don't you get bored?" Somewhere in our cockamamy cultural history we of the West decided boredom is bad. The simple and regenerative act of doing nothing became evil idleness, a condition leading straight to Hell. Dogs and fish and cows and horses, in their natural state, never are bored. If they have eaten and chased the mare around for a bit and dutifully peed around their territory (females obviously have their own agendas) they lie down and take a snooze, read a good book, or, if of a mind, play chess with the pigs.

Boredom is a peculiarly post-Luther, Western concept, the effect of which is to keep all of us deep in busy-ness if not in satisfying accomplishment. The end effect of Fear of Boredom is to drive us spinning to our graves and preventing us from looking down new paths lest there be nothing to do there.

There is, of course, plenty to do on a small boat crossing a large ocean. The "what to do" is survival, all those endless little tasks that allow your puny little vessel to deal with that scary big ocean. You repair and you mend and you plot your course. You spend a good deal of time decoding the sky for hints of what is ahead. You cook and you clean and you stand watch and steer the boat. You change sail and you reef and you endlessly check fittings and all those vulnerable places where a boat comes together and tries to fly apart.

Since the boat is your territory there is no need to pee around it, but you might spend a pleasant morning chasing a filly around the deck or, more likely, find her chasing you. You might even read a book. But never, never are you bored. You have a total, complete and closed universe to make work. You've never heard of God being bored, so why should you be?

The other side of all this activity at sea is that doing nothing, absolutely nothing, is wonderful. After depleting your adrenalin and fatiguing your muscles, two hours of lazily cataloging clouds hardly is boring.

The other fears, of sinking, of drowning, of collision at sea, of running out of food and water and of being struck down by appendicitis do not have nearly the force of Disappearance and Boredom. Those even non-sailors take in their stride. They are the acceptable risks.

The Big Two fears are firmed up on land and quickly dissipated at sea. The medium is the cure. But there is a third terror that comes upon the sailor at sea, the Fear of Bogeymen. While he learns to live with it and control it, the terror remains, if not during waking moments, then in nightmares.

There is nothing more spooky than being alone in the cockpit of a small boat on a starless, moonless night, with the wind howling from Hell and the seas trying to drive you there. All succumb to the Fear of Bogeymen. All feel the cold creep of antediluvian monsters up our back. On a wild night at sea we are all children in the dark—helpless children without a Mommy.

The absolute worst happened to a brave lady on a transatlantic crossing on my, too small by her standards, thirty-two footer. It was the first night out and, as usual, the wind and seas were up. Emmay had never before been to sea, never before that cold, dark night been on a sailboat. The winds had become steady and the forecast was for constant weather. So, in need of sleep, I put her out in the night, alone on her first watch. She was petrified but spunky as she huddled out there not quite knowing what to expect.

She was cold and frightened. She was sure she would do something stupid and sink the boat. No moon and no stars broke the pitchy black when she came out on watch at midnight. She sat huddled at the stern, hand cramped to the tiller. Little by little the feeling came over her that she was not alone in this vast darkness. Images of fearsome beings leaning over her shoulder grew until she was rigid with fear. The watch was three hours. One had already gone, only two more to go.

Suddenly, from inky darkness, the whole boat was lit up with a cold and eerie light. It had to be a monster rising up out of the sea, whose eyes cast that unearthly light. For a full minute she waited, in a cold sweat, for the touch of the monster and her terrible end. It was an eternal minute. From somewhere she summoned up the strength to turn. The suspense was simply too much.

The unearthly light was a full moon breaking, startlingly, through the clouds.

She shook for half an hour. The moon hid again behind the clouds and, in the darkness, her goblins started once more to come aboard. But having survived that blast of light, what else could happen?

And then one of the unseen monsters looming over her shoulder reached out a slimy, stinking, wet and cold paw and slapped her hard in the face. She screamed and fainted dead away.

On that black night this most recent of novices, already

terrified by moon and boat and imagined goblins, had taken a large flying fish full in the face. I can not imagine anything more terrifying.

Emmay took the wheel again the next night, and in the course of the passage took rein on her fears and proved a fine sailing companion. The Primal Fear had come and gone for her. The worst had happened and she had survived.

And so will you, my landlocked friend, so will you.

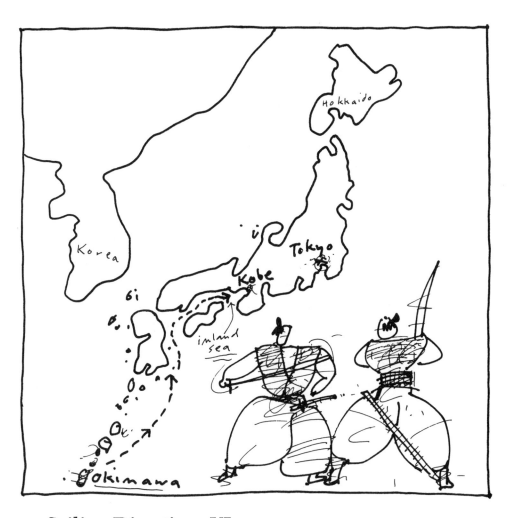

Sailing Directions VI

Before departing Okinawa toward Japan the base meteorologists will be delighted to pick a typhoon-free window for you. Use it for the dash to the island of Myajima. There you will be adopted by swarms of rich Japanese sailors, who will dine and wine and gift you like a visiting Shogun. Thence sail northwards toward Kobe in the misty Inland Sea. Check in at the Kansai Yacht Club and ask for Myakawa San, an ancient gentleman, secretary of the club, whose eye for

45

sweet little buttercups is only exceeded by his passionate need to serve you. Stay a year. If the typhoons don't sink you the weight of the gifts piled aboard by the frantic Japanese will. An American sailboat is a scarce item in Japan and the rich Japanese all are sailors. (In Japan, sailing is very chic.) There is little, including hara-kiri and immolation that they will not do for you. Makes you feel great at first. Gets a little itchy after awhile.

To get a true feel of Japan stay out of Tokyo. It is too much of endlessly the same thing. It is Levittown with slanty eyes. Get north into the mountains or, since you are there on a sailboat, cruise the Inland Sea. Not much wind but the small fishing villages that dot the shores take you back half a millenium. The only thing missing is a Samurai lopping off heads.

Japan is a manicured, color-coordinated country, wonderful to visit for a year but I'm glad I was not born there.

7

Picking a Crew

We are, each of us, our own best friend. We view ourselves, on balance, as approaching an ideal to which others should aspire. We tend to accept our attitudes, thoughts, ideas and emotional reactions as the preferred norms.

We rarely condemn ourselves and when we do there always is a convenient pillow of rationale upon which to recline our troubled egos. Manipulation and denigration of self are the exception rather than the rule and we usually are rather pleased with what we say or think. We are our own best company. When we choose others to keep us company —in our boats, our homes or even in our offices—they hardly can be such fine fellows as we know ourselves to be.

Whether, indeed, we are or are not fine fellows is not important. What is important is that we perceive ourselves to be so. What we think about ourselves, our sense of self worth, goes a long way towards making us what we are. If that be true, could not what we think about others also help them to be as swell as we ourselves are?

We think of others as having a pleiad of characteristics, acceptable or unacceptable to ourselves. Are they dependable? Do they talk too much? Are they shirkers? How about their emotional stability? (To all these questions please add one more. Are you?) We seem to think that people come in neat packages of personality traits. We then cast about to find the correct arrangement that satisfies our expectations.

If we subscribe to the perception of ourselves as being the cat's pajamas, then the excellence of our own package of qualities should be as evident to everyone else as it is to us. Alas, it does not seem to work that way. Each person in the world simply does not consider each other person the sterling character that each considers himself to be. People are not a concrete and objective package of qualities that add up to good or bad.

The truth is we live amidst a bewildering array of perceptions, none of which conform to everyone's standards. When we view others we do so from a foundation in the quicksand of convenience, compromise and prejudice.

What has all this to do with choosing a crew with whom it is possible to coexist on a long passage? The answer goes beyond choosing into the more lordly realm of causing to happen. Since the qualities of a crewmate depend on our perception of them, we are in the position to create an ideal crew. All we need is to perceive them as perfect and they become perfect.

Many of us snore and yet snoring, especially on a small boat, is considered bad form. Snoring tends to drive snorees right up the bulkhead even though the snoree might himself have been the snorer a moment earlier. We know we snore ourselves but we perceive (there's that word again) our snoring as being occasional, somewhat amusing and certainly not intrusive, even when it swells to such a strangulated volume as to wake us up.

If this is our perception of our own snoring, is it not possible, and preferable, to perceive other people's snoring in exactly the same manner? As occasional, amusing, and nonintrusive? Since we do not disapprove of it in ourselves, how sensible it would be to extend to our crewmates the same level of permissiveness that we enjoy ourselves.

The road to antipathy begins with our dislike for the act of snoring. The next step, which we all take, is to perceive our crewmate's snore as an aggressive act to keep us awake. We then shift distaste into the higher gear of hatred and thence onto the snorer, who remains peacefully asleep and unaware of the terrible processes going on in our brain. When the poor innocent awakes he finds himself under siege. Not knowing why he is being attacked, his defenses go up and now there are two people out of control, neither of whom is even approximately clear about the process that led them to their present contretemps.

In a small boat over a long passage, almost anything anybody does can become annoying. From annoying it escalates to aggravating and, presto, there is a destroyed voyage and a short-circuited friendship. On a small boat we are asked to deal, in endless contiguity, with personal confronts and affronts, which in ordinary, less cramped circumstances would be perceived as OK.

I suggest we must accept the character of our crewmates as given. It does not make any sense not to, since you can't change them. Decide that the qualities that are obnoxious to you do not, automatically, make your mate a bad person. We create obnoxious people by labeling their traits obnoxious. Unfair!

Good crewmates are people of whom you approve. It is

your act, not his or her qualities. If you grant your unreserved approval, you will find that even their most obnoxious idiosyncracies will lose focus in the gentle glow of your affirmation.

The picking of a crew is the skipper's prerogative. He has the opportunity to create a good crew by awarding generalized approval. Although it is the answer to the Bligh Syndrome, the award of approval is too infrequently used in crew selection. Here are a few simple guidelines for skippers wishing (as we all do) for comradeship and order on our passages.

1) Choose a crewperson. Use any criteria that will satisfy you. It does not matter what the criteria are. It is only important that the choice be full and free and complete.

2) Choose what you have chosen. Actively and willingly accept the choice that, after all, you have created. Retain no reservations. Cast out considerations.

3) Like what you have chosen. During the initial choosing process you can not always get what you like. Perhaps your requirements were too high or the group from which you were choosing was too small. (Perhaps it is made up of only one person . . . AHA!) Although you may not like the selection from which you have to choose, you can always, after the choice has been made, decide to like what you have chosen. If you persist in disliking your choice then there is nothing but disquiet and turmoil ahead for both you and your choosee. Decide, affirm and understand that, whatever comes up, you must now like your choice. It would be pretty dumb of you, otherwise.

Sophistry and paradox? No, a perfectly reasonable process. Start by admitting that the person you have chosen is much the same as you, for if you look closely you will find his character mirrored not only in yourself but, to a greater or lesser extent, in every other human being. Why waste energy in fighting the inevitable? Recognize you have, along with the multitudes living and dead, all those same qualities. Since you choose not to dislike them in yourself, then why not choose to like them in others? Develop the same affectionate regard for your crewmembers' taints as you have for your own.

We instructors during my war were instructed as follows: "First ya tell 'em what your gonna tell 'em. Then ya tell 'em what ya told 'em." Convinced by my own argument of the universality of bad habits, I consider necessary the following recapitulation:

A. Set up a series of considerations for and against any prospective crewperson.

B. Think about the considerations. Put a little pile of considerations on the good side and a little pile on the bad side of this choice. Then make a choice. The way your head works, this choice is very little affected, if at all by your struggle with consideration. The choice could, and does, go either way.

C. Accept your choice. It is completely irrelevant what choice is made. It is highly relevant and crucially important that you now accept, fully accept, the choice that you, yourself, have created.

D. Learn to like your choice. Liking is, after all, more satisfying than not liking. Unless you are a little weird in the head and quite perverse, you should choose liking over the negative and disquieting not liking.

Maybe you think the process just described is a bit efforted, somewhat far fetched and not relevant to the real world. If so, consider the procedure by which the most significant choice our society has to make is accomplished.

Selecting candidates for medical school is important, relevant and significant. In the selection and training of our physicians we define a good deal of the ease and comfort of our inevitable futures. Much, much thought has gone into this matter. Committees, interviews, board reviews, tests, past records and present appearance are all part, in varying proportions, of the selection process. The process reduces the multitude of applicants to the chosen few by no perceivable, consistent policy. Each school lends its own weight to the variegated elements of consideration.

The medical schools of America agree on only one thing in the selection and training process: They choose to like their choices. The result is that, once selected, a student finds it impossible to flunk out. The schools are so enamored of their selection mechanism they can not conceive that their chosen should do anything but succeed.

The barriers to failure are formidable. Retesting, tutoring, the repeating of years, study habit regimens and plain and simple intense peer pressure harry the unfortunate student who seems to be bored, lazy or stupid. What affirmation, what support, what approval! Through this curious process are selected and trained the acknowledgedly finest physicians in the world. If the system works for anything so portentous as medical education it should certainly work as well, or better, in the small matter of selecting crew.

This trilogy of choosing, accepting and liking is the only possible modus vivendi for a small sailboat. And since a small sailboat is no less a universe than the Universe itself, just maybe this is the way to get along in life. If you choose not to like what you have chosen you will be faced with the reality that the monster you are sailing (living, working) with is a monster of your creation. Liking and not liking is all in your head, generated, most probably, by little squirts of chemicals, the pipettes of which you can not control. While you can not casually direct these squirts, you can observe them, censor them and moderate them. You are, if not the captain of your own soul, at least its bosun.

The formula for avoiding bad voyages is to perceive your crew as you would have them perceive you. As Captain Rabbi Hillel said, "All else is commentary."

Sailing Directions VII

Depart Japan after leaving a sealed envelope in the hands of the U.S. embassy. The enclosed note gives full information of your vessel and crew and reveals that you sailed for Communist China without a visa. When you get to the mouth of the Yangtze open some seams in your main and ask for entry under protest. The Chinese are wonderful. I can think of no other word. Just wonderful. They will confer for days and try to find a precedent. But they don't even know what a

55

yacht is (and don't want to admit it). They will allow you a few days for repairs in Shanghai.

Sail up the Yangtze, truly yellow, and 50 miles or so upriver the water will turn dark. That is the mouth of the Huang Poo which, 20 miles further on, divides the heart of Shanghai. They will find someplace for you to tie up, will give you a 24-hour guard (to keep their people away not to keep you in) and if you are very polite, and insistent, they will allow you to look around. Buy silk material at one dollar the square meter.

Playing God

It has been convincingly argued that each of us is actually all the God there is in the Universe. If there is no God then the whacky human spirit in us, in postulating a God, actually becomes the Creator.

But we do not get much fun out of being Creator. It is a pointless exercise, be it true or not, which has little edible cheese. Being God and not knowing it lacks all the drama and excitement of playing God. Additionally, there are few opportunities to safely play God, since all of our peers would collapse in laughter and head us towards the nearest booby hatch the instant the game is made public.

It is night. You are seated in the stern alongside the wheel, which is wandering back and forth in answer to the urgings of the self-steering vane. You sit to starboard in the cockpit, the weather side, the high side. Your back is jammed against as many plastic float cushions as you can gather under you. Your legs are stretched out to the portside seat, locked and braced against the thrusting and intermittent seas slamming against the boat twelve inches from your back. The cushions slightly interdict the jolt of the coaming as the stern rises to steep, uneven, ten-foot seas.

Foul weather gear, open at the throat, stops some of the cold salt spray. The occasional solid dollop of sea water hits you as it is snatched by the wind from the tops of the seas running alongside. The water is cold and the salt bites, but the night is too warm to seal up your waterproof gear. So you suffer the insult of the sea on your neck and down along your chest. You also are getting wet beneath the tightly cinched belt of your bibbed pants. Salty sweat is gathering, irritatingly, between your legs. You have never been more uncomfortable in your life nor more sure that, above all else, you are where and how you want to be.

You can not see the companionway hatch seven feet away as there is no sky, just low cloud cover. The moon has already set in the west. With affection, you remember last night's stars, shedding enough starlight to see the bow and beyond. Tonight, without stars, without light, with companions dead asleep below, you are all the sentience there is. You are alone in the midst of an ocean which, for all you know, has no shores. Your horizon, if you could see it, is a scant three miles away. Your universe is a circle of sea only six miles across. You realize that whatever there is beyond those few miles—if there is anything beyond, your bemused mind seems to say—has no relevance in your personal universe. You are alone, and on watch.

God is not easy to play. He is well known to do mostly either nasty things or nice things. To play God you would have to copy his style. It is not much fun to play God doing either nothing or doing the same old things that you do every day, anyway. It is unfortunate that those few occasions when folk do get to play God, are occasions in which the drama lies in dolling out bad news and worse events. When you hear the comment, "He's playing God," it usually means that somebody is about to do something perfectly awful to somebody else. It is almost impossible, and would be very dull, to write a reasonable, workable scenario for playing a God doing nice things.

It is three o'clock in the morning and your vessel is a thousand leagues offshore with another thousand to go before reaching safe harbor. The heavens have begun their darkest wheel towards the west. Sunrise will be on your watch. You will accomplish the dawn just as if you caused the sun to rise. For your mates sleeping below the safe reappearance of the sun is indeed the gift of your attention to the countless acts of protection lavished on the boat all night long.

You listen for a change in the sound of the water rushing along your side. You strain to hear the rhythm of the seas that come at you in a steady march from the same direction. You test the tension of the lines holding your sails, steel-bar tight as they take the thrust of the wind. You listen always and forever for the telltale semidemiquaver of wind that might forewarn an ominous change. You watch the horizon for lights that should not be there, and if, among the empty vastness of the sea, a light should devilishly appear, it is your passionate duty to determine its direction and speed and avoid a collision.

From your vantage point in this infinite inky darkness—much like the space Gods must live in—you listen to the familiar and comforting creak of the boat telling you in its rubbings that all is well, or with an unfamiliar ping, that all is not well. You check the bilges for a suspicious inch of water that should not be there. You smell the air for rain and you wish for the moon so you might use her to map the shape of your clouded sky.

You check your compass and check it again and again. You make sure that some sleepy soul did not leave a piece of errant iron close enough to warp its pointing. Each hour you record speed, wind speed and direction and estimated distance traveled in careful dead reckoning. And just before your watch is over and you must reenter mortality, you strap on the safety harness and make just one more circumnavigation of the deck, feeling in the dark for any untoward development that might endanger your charge.

On a sailboat on a blue-water passage this is the one transcendent, magical moment during which each crewmember has Godlike power over his mates. During these delicious hours, when standing watch, he is as close to Godhead as any sailor, and much, much closer than any landbound creature ever will be. During his watch the future of every soul on board is in his keeping. The lives of his crewmates are his to protect or destroy.

It is the moment of deepest responsibility. A moment when you know, without reservation, that your actions mean something. It is then you know your existence is real and purposeful and not some empty stochastic accident.

Is this not the way God does it? Is not His chiefest function to spread an umbrella of care and concern over His unknowing, unconscious and subsentient subjects just as you spread yours? Does He not stand watch just as you do?

As you watch your subjects sleep, praying you their souls to keep, you truly are playing God. You are drunk with the power of your loneliness and exalted by your care for your fellows, who have anointed and sanctified you by their trust.

And if there should be no God to imitate, then you are, for these three magical hours, the real, the true, and the only God your mates will ever have.

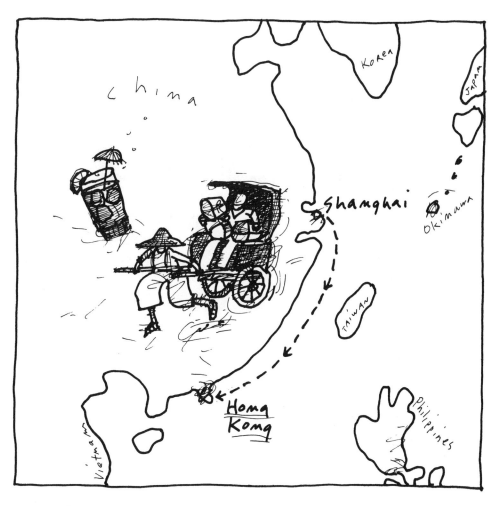

Sailing Directions VIII

From Shanghai head south towards Hong Kong. HK is a place where you will find six shops in each block, each one selling everything that you want at prices that make discount catalogs look silly. Check in at the Royal Hong Kong Yacht Club for a berth and a whiff of Empire. It's home of the best, the very best, bar in the world.

Then go buy stuff. Any HK sailmaker will do you a set, in tanbark if you like, for a fifth of US prices. (Try Lee Sailmak-

ers—ask for Helen.) If you are a stainless steel freak, carry your magnet about and find fasteners and even stainless anchors and chain. Miss nothing mechanical for westward from HK, except for insipid Singapore, is an industrial desert.

Try to avoid the pirates at the entrances to HK. They prey mostly on bigger boats but on a slow day they might nibble on you. Any determined display of your intention to defend yourself will discourage them. Pirates they may be—brave pirates they ain't.

9

Wives and Lovers

In bad weather, one of the women aboard invariably is at the helm or soon finds her way there. The women do not cause the bad weather (a theory passionately held in earlier times). It is the other way about, the bad weather conjures up a female hand. It is a time to sit in awe and watch the ladies handle shitty seas and violent winds.

One lady, whose soul is full of music, does not steer the boat, she dances with it. Her body undulates and bounces as if driven by a rhythm unheard by the males aboard. Her concerns stretch beyond direction and course into a more elemental relationship with wave and wind. She becomes part, as only a woman can, of the femaleness of the sea. Where I fight the wheel, she caresses and accommodates it. Where I view the sea as antagonist, it is to her a nurturing of her own biological directives. She steers with her ovaries, not with her hands.

She deals with discomfort at the wheel as women deal with pain in childbirth—a condition given, not subject to either complaint or amelioration. In her best moments, she told me, cold and wet and more than a little in terror of the unknown, she enters into a warming and thoughtless symbiosis with ship and sea. At that moment she is complete, and both ship and sea are she. It's a closed circle of condition that no man can ever approach but that women always do in the secret femaleness of their lives with us.

Men rarely understand women, never understand wives and, only in the most imperfect sense, perceive their own function in relationship to what certainly is the older sex. I can not conceive of male preceding female since reproduction of cells is by division of self and self in the act of procreation always is female. In nature's eyes we all must have been female in the beginning and perhaps well beyond.

Just why the primal mother sex, which so clearly dominated the early evolution of our race, chose to give up their control to Johnny Come Lately is the source of some of the mystery surrounding women even to this day. The male lament that starts with, "If I live to be a hundred . . ." commenced with his bewilderment at being anointed by women to be his ruler.

Women's consent to be ruled is inherent in a conscious female perception that ruling is a feckless and exhausting pursuit, not nearly worth the candle of life it consumes. A male friend, deeply engrossed in his rabbi's disputes with his flock, complained that synagogue politics are so bitter, "because the stakes are so small." A woman perceives that the real stakes, even of ruling the whole world are, in a teleological sense, infinitely small, while the stakes involved in giving birth to even one child is teleology itself. The battlegrounds of government may be wider, but, in a real sense, the stakes of ruling the world are no larger than the stakes involved in who shall be the chosen to sit by the east wall. As if God cares.

In the business of living from day to day, women loom large on the horizon of maleness. Despite their biological originality we are required to rule them, although the cachet of leadership is their gift. We males, all, look up to our women, and the only way we can deal with their insufferably evident superiority is, from our vantage point below, to look up their skirts. This concupiscent view of women has given us a certain lusty resemblance of control and has caused to be built the strained and tenuous structures of modern male societies.

In looking up to women, a view that reveals more of their pubes than their potential, we build societies of lies. We tell the lies and our ladies swear to them out of their lack of predeliction for power. In accepting from their hands the mantle of their dominance we become not their masters but their slaves. We are no more than a mechanism for allowing them the unencumbered pursuit of a mysterious and essentially female biological imperative. Unlike boy spiders we do not get eaten. But we are denied the sensory and emotional structures required to complete our humanity. Surrounded as we are by a humus of high class ladies, all vibrating at a sensual level that we can not reach, we, the males, are erotically déclassé.

This view of maleness illuminates life at sea. Early sailors were denied women aboard (I can not imagine why) so they transferred denial into the belief that distaff presence guaranteed an unlucky passage. Despite this suspicion of women aboard, they invariably named their boats after women. The bowsprit, an inescapably Freudian projection, grew beneath it a figurehead of a woman with either bared or at least emphasized breasts. Boats were paradigms for the banished sex. They became personified, sensual, female objects evoking love and self-sacrifice. Women, even in their absence, had again carried the battle.

Perhaps it is because of this paradox that the matings of a small boat sailor are clearer and more satisfying than those he has ever had on land. At sea the roles of the protagonists are more sharply defined and the clatter of the extraneous is dulled. Encouraged by the enforced sharing of duties by both sexes, the need for roles of ruled and ruler is less critical.

Even on land she has qualities you can only perceive when you stop looking up her skirts. When she is sick she is stoic. When you are sick she ministers to you with an affectionate dedication that gives the word "nurse" its gender. She is calm in emergencies and when danger appears she panics less than you do. (Hysteria, punatively a woman's disorder, was invented by women to force reluctant males to function.) She lets her orgasms flow rather than splurt. The human race has achieved more from the slow and measured release of its passions and its strengths than ever it did from spastic eruption.

At sea, if you are stupid, you try to force upon her the role of cook and washer up. If you are wise you accept your own share of galley and latrine duty, help her to break the self-imposed bonds of false ineptitude in "man's" work, and thus reinforce your lust for her with a companion's love. If she is stupid she continues the charade of your superiority that she has created and, not recognizing the altered needs and circumstances of being at sea, cheats herself of knowing herself —and you—better.

If she be wise in the way of humankind, and most women cannot avoid that sort of perception, then she will seek out the change that makes whole people of both you and her.

Thus at sea the game of male superiority is no longer played with impunity. The burden of rulership fades. On a small boat the female acquiescence of an inferior position to avoid the burden of being in charge is dispelled apace. Women created us as their surrogate rulers . . . at sea the surrogacy lacks function. Radical cultural realignment becomes de rigueur.

So, Mr. Skipper, unless you are prepared to abdicate some of your more dearly (and falsely) held images of self and unless you are also able to change the way you strut your stuff, keep your boat male. But if you do keep only men about you, you will miss most of the fun of having delightfully revealed your lady's, and your own, true and natural selves.

When you finally decide to integrate (some would say complete) your crew, be aware that you are mucking about with elemental biological forces. Be prepared to accept the whirlwind of passion and life that will, if you are lucky, be released from the pressure cooker gestalt of a modern woman. Offer her the love and the sex of a colleague, rather than the false control of inherited kingship. Your life will never be dull and you will spend much less time wondering, intellectually, what you are doing on this Earth. She, released, will share her furies with you until you learn, as she has, that the wellspring of understanding lies not in the middle of your medulla but in the middle of your gut. You will share the throne of life with her as colleague, sister, mistress and wife. The Pharaohs knew, at least the ones who married their sisters did.

Should you take a woman to sea on a long passage, you embark upon a splendid adventure that goes far beyond the thrills of wind and wave and exotic ports. By allowing her aboard and by allowing the uncluttered emotional breeze of a sea voyage to blow through your relationship, you are inviting your boat and the sea and your woman to finally and at last make a man of you.

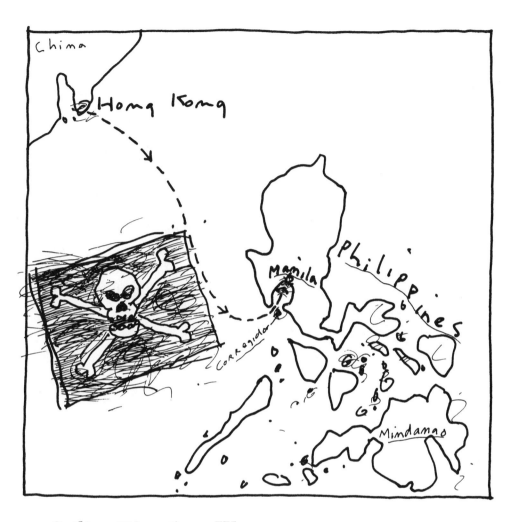

Sailing Directions IX

After departing Hong Kong sail towards the Republic of the Philippines, home of the loveliest cruising grounds on Earth, also complete with pirates. A thousand lush islands spread out for your delectation. The enclosed and protected waters make the Caribbean look anemic. Some islands are dotted with villages of the most innocent and attractive inhabitants. Some islands are unexpectedly unpeopled. All are beautiful.

69

Because Philippine politics lie just to the right of Genghis Khan, the large island of Mindanao is in control of insurgents who support themselves by attacks on shipping. It's understandable when you get to know the governing classes. But real piracy exists at Corregidor at the entrance to Manila Bay and, you better believe it, in the bay and harbor itself. All very disturbing, but the place is not to be missed.

Check in at the Manila Yacht Club where cheap native labor repays us for carrying the white man's burden. In the Philippines you can have anything done for a buck, or get to do anything to anybody for two bucks. A place of deep, and cheap, deviation. Stay a year and look around for Rowdy on the most disreputable-looking trimaran in the China Sea. If he is away cruising he will be back soon.

10

Wheedling, Or, As Long As You Are Going Below Anyway, Would You Mind Building The Taj Mahal?

Wherever you happen to be on a lurching, leaping sailboat is better than any other place you might be on the boat. You could be half under water, half drowned, half frozen and wholly miserable and still the prospect of relocation daunts.

To be anywhere else on a sailboat, rather than precisely where you are, requires that you move. And movement is (1) what you've got too much of already and (2) hurts.

If you can imagine the comfortable room that you now inhabit developing a 20-degree tilt and alternately trying to fling you out of your seat or slamming you back into it, and all the while having cold water fulminating into your face, you might get a slight sense of how most sailors feel most of the time. If you add to all this the embarrassing fact that all sailors (including me and only excepting those with inner ear anomalies) are endemically seasick, you begin to get the full flavor of the madness of sailing.

Manipulative Wheedling is the Black Commandment,

which states, "Thou shalt do naught for thyself that you can wheedle others into doing for you." The MW practitioner is a parasite upon his crewmates. He contributes nothing to their lives, except perhaps to expand and enhance their inclination to paranoia. Parasite is a better term than symbiont. Leech is perhaps the best. A leech in spider's clothing.

The sly and experienced maritime manipulator expands leagues beyond the simple, "Would you mind bringing me a soda when you come on deck?" Only a beginner would be so churlishly obvious. The sophisticated practitioner of high level MW has been known to achieve an entire passage without once getting out of his bunk (naturally the warmest and driest on the boat).

On land, while frowned upon, MW is not as despicable as it is at sea. In the comfort of your own warm living room you may be watching your favorite sitcom and do not want to miss a predictable moment of high drama and low libidiousness. Your mate rises gracefully from her soft chair (to which it is not necessary to be tied) and heads toward the fridge. Under these felicitous circumstances, it is entirely permissible to call, "Bring me a beer when you come back, Hon." That's no big deal.

But on a sailboat it is a big deal. Try this scenario. It is night and it is 3:30 in the morning and it is cold. The boat is beating into a nasty little chop dealing indiscriminate boat bites to anyone not totally horizontal and perfectly padded. You and your watchmate have just come on deck coerced by an insane and irrational sense of duty to abandon warm and dry bunks for a cold and wet cockpit. (If your watchmate happens also to be your bedmate you may have exchanged a literal cockpit for a lousy one.)

Upon being called by the impatient watch you are relieving, you have had to go through the exhausting Tai Chi of finding and donning stiff, cold and damp foul weather gear.

To make matters worse (if that is possible) the vagaries of the sea and the laws of physics prevent arm and armhole and leg and leghole from being in the same spot at the same time. Insertion becomes a problem. The best two-word description of dressing on a moving sailboat is, thrust and hope.

After an agonizing eternity, you complete your preparations and relieve the old watch, now frantic and furious at your delay. Your first Manipulation of the night has been achieved. You have cheated them out of half an hour of sleep.

The shock of being on deck, awake, cold and sick leaves you numb and uncaring—for a while. As life returns, you realize you want a hot chocolate. You would really like a hot chocolate. You would love a hot chocolate. You would, in fact, kill for a hot chocolate. But the merest suggestion that you might find yourself moving about the boat is so horrifying that self-service is unthinkable.

So, like a spider, you lie in wait for a victim. You watch, as well as you can in the dark, the only person other than yourself who can accomplish your hot chocolate—your innocent watchmate.

He is the only available possibility. You have wisely dismissed a desperate plan to cry "man overboard," and rouse the boat. In the ensuing confusion and the general relief of finding all accounted for (all being then on deck), you thought you might be able to do a quick wheedle on somebody. However, you reason correctly that the offwatch might very likely see through your ploy and effect a real man overboard, namely you. After this flight of fancy you revert to an intense, feral and singleminded observation of your target of opportunity.

Your partner sits across from you with a different sort of problem. He (or she) has just become aware, with disbelief, of the growing and imperious need to make caca. No small matter on a boat, especially if the caca-er happens to be

chronically constipated and a bowel movement represents a
long wished-for development. "But why," the poor unfortunate asks despairingly, "Why just now?"

The signals have been ignored for a while, but the message
becomes increasingly clear and strident. There is simply no
way your watchmate can wait the four hours for relief (in
both senses). Having just struggled into his foul weather gear
he is now faced with the heartsickening prospect of struggling out of them.

To get out of his clothes, he must first get below. Since the
motion is heavy, the list severe and the deck slippery, he is
aware that the boat will abuse him unmercifully as he clam-
bers, crawls and lurches toward the head. The boat seems in
league with his bowels.

You hang patiently in your web, sensing that your moment
is approaching. Your partner's groans precede his actual un-
harnessing. His whimpers accompany the tearing of his fin-
gernails as he claws his way to the companionway hatch.
You watch him, unremittingly, knowing that a badly timed
wheedle, just a nanosecond too soon, will cause him to fall
back and settle for cramps, constipation and a bad head-
ache.

So you wait until he has invested too much energy and
pain to turn back. Just as his head disappears below, you call
out blithely and with exquisite timing, "As long as you're
below, mind bringing me a hot chocolate? There's some in
the thermos."

Now you know damn well there is no hot chocolate in the
thermos, but you are betting he doesn't. By the time he discovers this he will be so deeply entangled in your web he is
lost, a defeated wheedlee. He slowly realizes he is being
wheedled. He had fought his way to the head, struggled out
of his clothes and sat developing a monumental fury at falling
into your trap. And now, to add debasing insult to debilitating injury, he realizes that, in most imperfect justice, his

anger has shut off his bowels. The whole painful exercise has come to naught.

He must now struggle back into his recalcitrant gear, fight his way forward to the galley and burn himself, on his way up on deck, with your lousy hot chocolate. He cleanses his mind of the horror that nature might again prevail in an hour or so and the whole mortifying business require repeating.

This is the moment he discovers that the thermos is empty and what had begun as an insulting service now requires (oh, my God, no!) that water be boiled. The stove must be lit, requiring both nauseating alcohol and kerosene, water must be pumped and the chocolate powder found. The powder is, of course, buried deeply behind heavy cans and jars (which is why the thermos was empty in the first place).

He has been bested, totally defeated, in that most ancient form of naval warfare, the first salvo of which always is the innocuous broadside, "As long as you are. . . ."

And you, you despicable insect, still unmoved from your cozy cockpit corner and further unmoved by the pain, and degradation of your mate, will get your hot chocolate. Probably not even poisoned.

Like many an opera bouffe, this one really happened . . . and to me. I was the constipated one. I lurched about with the empty thermos. I boiled the water. I was seasick and made even more sick by kerosene and alcohol. I tasted the dregs of defeat.

And then the next night, with a slight but brilliant variation, the bastard got me again. But I struck back. This time "by mistake" I made the hot chocolate from the seawater tap.

The passage was ruined. Our friendship was ruined. The chocolate was ruined and my bowels were ruined.

Sailing Directions X

From the Philippines your way is clear to the island of Borneo, and its baby Sultanates. Sail along the north coast, the south shore is ungoverned. Whip down to Bali, if you like, for disappointment and arrogant officialdom, (sailors are not welcome) and thence to Singapore, the dullest place in creation. It is neat and clean and impeccably governed. The

77

prices are cheap and if you jaywalk or spit in the street a polite and unbribable policeman appears to fine you. Lots of cruising sailors. But dull.

—11——

Gurgitation

How sailing ever got to be a popular voluntary activity is one of the larger of life's smaller mysteries. Take any ten people, sailors and/or non-sailors, it makes no never-mind, and talk to them of the delights of sailing.

Tell them about beautiful people, about exotic places, desert islands, escape from deadening routine. Talk about health, vitality, long life and cute hats. Watch as their eyes light up. See them salivate. Watch the envy grow. Listen as they start computing the things they can sell so they can join you before it is too late.

Then take a different group of ten. Do not anesthetize them with visions of topless girls, bottomless men and the topless towers of Ilium. Try this word association test:

"What is the first thing that comes to mind when I say sailing?"

"Puke," nine out of ten answer. With that, you are near to the central paradox of sail and also to the human inclination to let small inconveniences interfere with large ecstasies.

This also raises the question of why puke is held in such disrepute. It is a learned, not an inherited, disgust. Watch any baby throw up. It is an easy, natural activity rewarding the infant with a relieved belly. Why can't we learn to love our vomit? I did, and therein lies a tale.

Nineteen fifty-one was a good year for the world and a good year for me. I was at the London School of Economics. The war and a respectable bachelor's degree were behind me. I had never yet been on a sailboat but Someone was thinking about it for me.

Europe was still swirling in confusion and reconstruction and had not yet fully organized the efficient extraction of cash from American tourists. Europe was cheap and Americans were all Rockefeller. Almost anything was within the financial reach of even a penurious student such as myself.

The gold rings at which I grasped were the storied restaurants of France. In that innocent summer, in a borrowed, topless, prewar MG, I wheeled into Dijon (a city just far enough away from Paris) accompanied by Dick Kelly, a man of high appetites and low humor. We asked directions to La Pyramide.

There are only a handful of three-star restaurants in France. The granting of stars by the Guide Michelin (published by the makers of rubber tires) is taken with sufficient seriousness to cause the suicide of chefs upon their withdrawal. Most of the trois-etoiles establishments are in Paris but a few, and on my tongue the best, lie in the countryside.

La Pyramide is one of these. It is a smallish place, open air in the summer, and was judged to have the best kitchen in France. It was toward these gustatory heights that I yearned and to which I had dragged poor Dick Kelly. We arrived by accident at 8:30 in the evening, the most proper hour to dine in France. After we groveled a bit and cleaned our eyeglasses with twenties, they agreed to feed us.

I remember nothing of the meal save that it was superb. It was constructed of eight courses, each cleanly separated from the next by taste, color and texture, much like a parfait. Each course descended in lonely splendor and layered itself in my belly awaiting a signal from the chef to commence digestion. The mixing process was designed to start, I now know, when dessert was followed by coffee. The process was interdicted when I chose as dessert a glorious pastry that cleverly disguised the fact it was made mostly from almonds.

I am desperately allergic to almonds. As the pastry slipped down my gullet and gently plopped on top of the beautiful meal, I received an urgent autoimmune command to replace consumption with gurgitation. I obeyed and in the nicely decorated Louis Quatorze men's room I returned, in its entirety, the meal of the best restaurant in France. It reappeared in reverse order to its ingestion and each separate, glorious course came past my palate in an orderly progression. Each, due to the legerdemain of the chef, retained its original flavors and bouquets. An altogether delightful experience, like getting twice as much for your money. As an additional bonus, as if that were necessary, my gourmand guts were light and empty with only the perfect memory of a perfect meal, while Dick groaned and gurgled all night with indigestion. In unknowing anticipation of sailing days to come I had received my first lesson in loving my vomit.

When sailing days did arrive I was prepared to accept regurgitation (which curiously has a definition nearly identical to "gurgitation") simply as the reverse of ingestion, nothing pejorative implied. The large ecstasy I had discovered in sail was not to be snatched away by an environmentally imposed distaste for a natural function not entirely unlike an exhaled breath.

For the sailor, this tale carries two powerful lessons, which become relevant when you find yourself tossing your cookies, not in an elegant Sun King men's room in France, but over the wet and scary lee rail of a small boat in a large ocean.

It is a given that every meal you take on a small sailboat carries with it a mathematical probability you will find yourself whoopsing to lee. That knowledge is what keeps people out of sailing even more than all the used car salesmen who abusively try to sell them boats.

The second lesson is that if you are going to throw up anyway, put stuff down that will come up nicely. No need to suffer with the sour when with a little planning and forethought to taste, you can arrange for the second act to be almost as pleasurable as the first.

There lies an eternal truth here somewhere. It is evident from the vomitophobe's reaction that they see no further than their rising gorge and that the mere thought of vomiting makes them want to throw up. They exhaust themselves in disgusted anticipation; a coward pukes a thousand times, a brave man once. If they could but circle that thought and get to the act of sailing, they would vomit less and, like the return of my three-star meal, they would enjoy it more.

How many times, whilst attending to your needs in a men's room (is it any different in a ladies room?) have you heard a long drawn-out sigh followed by, "Taking a leak is the second best thing in the world." The inference is that the first best thing in the world is screwing and the third is shitting. Well, if we are clear that these three are so wonderful, who decided that vomiting isn't?

It is only a mind set, and like a clock it only needs resetting. It is easier and less taxing to love than to hate. Loving regurgitation, therefore is much more sensible than letting a little thing like a natural function close off peak life experiences.

Learn to love it all, nausea, vomiting, your boss, your job, Colonel Quaddafy and even your wife. When you do they will all go quietly away and let you enjoy your life at sea.

(Note to Editor: If I have to rewrite this one more time I may throw up.)

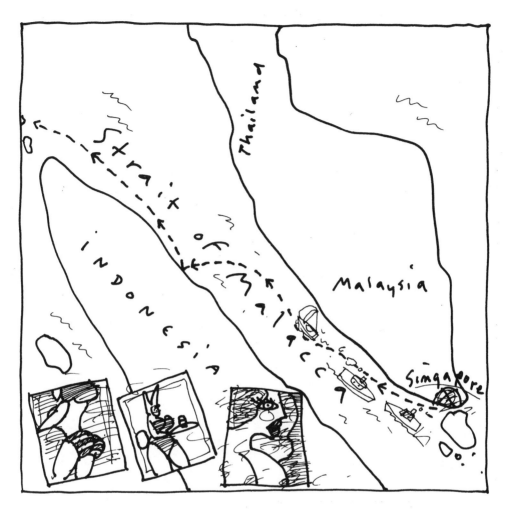

Sailing Directions XI

Sail north from Singapore up the fabled Straits of Malacca where all the busy traffic of the East passes that of the West. Cling close to the western shore (Indonesia), where there are no pirates, as there may be along the shores of Thailand. Try not to pause in Indonesia where all is confusion and the pettiest of officialdom. If you must stop there have plenty of issues of Playboy aboard. Do not pass out whole copies.

Hand each panting official a single page. Very effective bak-sheesh in Indonesia, where even Playboy's pallid pornography is banned.

—12—

Sea Change

On our first blue-water passage we are confronted with all of the abuse the sea saves for it's tyros. If that is not injury enough we also are expected to suffer the insult of seeing ourselves stripped naked of the coddling, cotton wool of land. Nothing is warm, nothing is dry, the boat bites at you with its lurchings and the next twenty days look like twenty years. An hour out and already we are toying with the question of why in the world we are out there. It is a question that we carefully avoid posing to ourselves as day after day the agony goes on and our embarrassment mounts at our foolishness for being at sea. Misery and confusion reach exponential heights and we await the disintegration that comes when our limits are reached.

We puke and sweat and suffer. We puke some more and drag ourselves out of the only pleasure left to us, sleep, to stand watch in a terrifying banshee blackness. We are sure we are lost. We feel alone, cut off from friends and family. Ease and comforts are only dimly remembered. We try to be brave, and our brave little egos deny us even the invalid degradation of an emotional breakdown—and the passage is not yet a quarter over.

At the very bottom of the pit, when each sense and sensibility is violated and raw with the abuse of motion and sea, when foolish hopes for early relief have long since joined dinners overboard, something begins to happen.

We become conscious of, if not relief from misery, an altered state. The misery begins to feel natural—almost sufferable. Our more experienced companions again take on individual personalities. Until now they had become merely things in our path to the rail or objects of the most profound hatred as they awakened us for our watch. Our eyes clear a bit and through a dimming haze of nausea we note that they function, are not nauseated, enjoy their food and even seem to be having fun. And with the first shred of hope we have felt for days, we realize that they, too, in their voyages must have suffered the same. And they have come back for more. Some kind of magic must be at work. Why should they expose themselves again to a state where death is a wished-for conclusion unless there is, indeed, an end to this gall and wormwood.

There is a curious moment when we pause in our retching and raise our eyes and, for just the briefest second, we see a hint of beauty in the wave that is trying to toss us over the rail. The moment is quickly buried as the wave comes alongside and slaps the vomit back into our mouth with cold, salt water. But the next day another moment happens—maybe two. And the next day another, and the passage suddenly is longer behind us than it is ahead.

A cracker becomes conceivable to swallow and unexpectedly our nostrils take some pleasure in the smell of the sea, replacing for a moment the sour vapors of vomit. We find all our movements do not end at the rail.

The time comes on a small boat, when the sufferer must either improve or die. It is then, if you have allowed it enough time, when the Sea Change, that mysterious reaccommodation of senses to the sea, occurs. Few die and almost no one never improves. Genetic memories remind your body that you are out of the sea only for a few billion years. With so recent an aquatic history why all the misery? What is all the fuss about? The Sea Change, so long yearned for, lies at the end of your long tunnel of nausea.

And then it happens. Against all logic, sick, bone-weary, frightened and abused, a vagrant, unimaginable thought from beyond the bounds of reason drifts through. You discover you are sorry that the passage is soon to end!

The defeat of nausea is only the beginning of the Sea Change. Your values alter. The importance of purely being is the goal of the Change and it starts by dealing with, and discarding, the hundred hurdles of discomfort that you weave around on land. Avoiding these hurdles is an exhausting process—using much more time and energy than it is worth. Part of the gift of the sea is the teaching that discomfort is acceptable, that pain is only the other side of pleasure. Suddenly you can reclaim the living that you once denied yourself only because it had to be bought with the coin of inconvenience.

Being at sea is all inconvenience. Nothing is easy on a small boat. To get to the larger delights, the Sea Change teaches us to ignore the smaller miseries.

On land you have developed an acute sense of your own aging. You are forced into the mold of what is the 'proper' attitude and image for your particular decade. You measure your life against some weird yardstick of what's left. Since you have more goals on land than you have life to live, the sense of "wasted time" destroys even the pleasure in time not wasted. At sea you are busy, asleep, awash in sensory delight or terrified, all good things to be. The Sea Change is that process by which a tight, constipated, beset and besotted sailor is given the opportunity to live. The Sea Change guarantees you love being busy, asleep, awash and terrified. You simply do not have the time to get old. The Sea Change offers you, at least while you are alive, a kind of immortality.

The Sea Change leaches out the acids of jealousy and competitiveness. You compete only with the sea itself and since it is a superior antagonist, the Sea Change teaches blessed acceptance. The Sea Change teaches the special joy of staying even, of living only in the precious now.

Sailing Directions XII

Coming around the northern tip of Indonesia you will pass a lighthouse that does not work and the port of Saban, which does not work, either. If you find yourself in Saban do absolutely nothing by the book and have plenty of Playboys ready. "By the book" to Indonesian officials means written reports and the certainty of bureaucratic retribution. Do not be too hard on them, they are just trying to save their asses. Immediately upon tying up locate someone to bribe, and keep bribing. They are not greedy or sophisticated in the ways of corruption and will be grateful and helpful if you don't ask them to do anything official.

13

Total Cleansing

You are different than you were seven years ago. You are, in fact, a totally new human being. You have changed your personality, you have matured, and you have managed to escape from the lovely innocence of youth. You have osmosed knowledge and acquired a broadened understanding of yourself and your fellows. Although all of these obvious changes have taken place they are only an adjunct to the subtle and unseen miracle that alters every human on earth every seven years.

Little wonder the number seven takes on magical properties. In each seventh year, every seventh year of our lives, through the intercession of TC we are totally remade. Total Cleansing, certainly the trickiest of nature's bag of tricks, involves the complete replacement of every body cell every eighty-four months. Skin, fat, bone, brain, liver, heart and all the rest, retain not one living cell nor one molecule today that existed in you seven years ago.

If this is not miracle enough, the memory of who we are and what we are and what we think and smell like and look like and what we remember has been preserved in these new cellular strangers. So, while we are altogether different, we remain absolutely the same.

Biologists and teleologists may have an explanation for this septennial replacement. Whatever faddish theory they have constructed, nature, for reasons of her own and to which we are not yet privy, has chosen periodically to totally cleanse us, to give us new life. The old, the tired and the corrupted parts of us are not allowed to remain to destroy us. They are thrown away and all new material is brought in from the outside for a Total Cleansing.

Nature's original plan presupposed there would be few enough of us on this wide Earth that always there would exist plenty of fresh, new material for her to use. The rub is she was somewhat too successful with us as a species. Now we are too many and very busily fouling up our planet home. Few places are left to us on our globe where there remain uncontaminated stuffs for our remaking.

Asbestos, radioactive residue, inimicable hydrocarbons, acid rains, pesticides, herbicides, airborne lead and mercury, and the whole miserable catalog of industrial turd has made nature's goal to renew us impossible.

Our industry and our assholes are everywhere slipping sewerage into the very stuff from which our new bodies are being made. Even our schools are laced with asbestos fiber. All about us the land is glowing, each day just a little more, with the undisposable refuse of our nuclear adventures.

The high and mighty, the lowly and poor, princes and paupers alike are all, except for sailors in the deep oceans, being remade with the stuff that ultimately will kill them.

In this generation the deep oceans still are clean. The pollutants have not yet been able to filter through a thousand miles of sea water a thousand fathoms deep. The air over the oceans still is clean. It is onto the suffering land that most pollutants are deposited. Total Cleansing still works at sea.

The ideal Total Cleansing is an offshore sailing passage of

seven years. If things become much more turgid on land, it is not impossible to anticipate that people, seeking air for emphysemic lungs, the clean water of a tropic rain shower and the food of the still unpolluted sea, will move, slowly but permanently, onto the sea in a new sort of sailing vessel. A vessel designed never to touch land. A vessel designed for life.

A far-fetched picture of the future? You know what is happening in the close-fetched picture. It would not be a bad life. We have the technology to create indestructible boats that can last for generations. With sail, the power requirements are minimal and we are fast approaching a solar conversion system that will give us the little electricity we need. We will not be alone. We can raft a thousand boats together, a new kind of tribe, with enough genetic variety to breed us some swell people. Out there no government can tax us or foolishly direct us to do things we know are both stupid and destructive. We can live on and below the sea in more luxury and more comfort, and at less cost than we are paying now in our money and in our health.

Sometimes one tends to overstate. And sometimes, perversely, the extravagance has enough truth and validity that your kids find themselves living in the very world of fantasy you invented. Perhaps they indeed will find the seas more congenial than a polluted land. But the point is not to urge you to sell the ranch and move to Sargasso Acres. Rather, it is to point out that, of all places, the deep oceans are the healthiest, and you damn well ought to be out there as much as you can.

The seven-year Total Cleansing is not the only health reason why the sea and a small sailing vessel should be everyone's lifestyle of choice. More immediate reasons exist for the sea life, such as the care and feeding of your existing body.

Life on land encourages heart disease and obesity. We all

are too lazy to exercise enough and too gluttonous to mount enough resistance to reverse the trend. Little fatty puddles accumulate in our aortas. We all need a total fitness program that attacks gluttony and encourages vigorous exercise. Not an easy matter, since the breaking of ancient eating habits and the agony of producing sweat are matters to which we are highly resistant. We need a fitness program that makes food unattractive and causes us to vigorously work our bodies without conscious knowledge that we are doing so. What we need are the indolent isometrics of a small sailing boat. What we need is the appetite discourager of nausea.

On a sailing vessel fat disappears soon enough under the triple threat of 1) eating less because you are slightly nauseous, 2) throwing up a lot when you are deathly nauseous and 3) burning fat off in the endless, tight-bellied isometric battle with the constant motion of the sea.

Do nothing and get thin. Sounds too good to be true? You bet your fat ass it is!

In fact, you bet much more than your ass, since along with kissing your supercallipygian poundage good-by, you also part with your cellulite, your middle tire, your wattles, your chins and other landlubberly flab produced by sloth and gluttony.

Isometric exercising has a peculiarly modern ring to it. The truth is this form of activity dates back to an antediluvian clam's struggle to open when sat upon by a fat fish. Isometrics are no more than straining muscles against some immovable object and the human race has had lots of practice in that.

But the real home of isometrics is every small sailboat. No matter whether it is tied to a dock, wallowing in an oily calm or flailing about in a wild sea, its occupants constantly are isometrically fighting motion.

Belly muscles are toned up by the retching over the lee rail and then kept in tone by the endless battle to keep torso reasonably perpendicular over hips. The beginning sailor may, at first, resent this abuse. But as his tummy flattens and as those lovely lines of limber muscle work themselves out through the fat, the nausea and the ceaseless tensioning and detensioning prove worthwhile.

A sometimes distaff plus of the ceaseless isometrics on a boat is the welcome lofting of breasts. As she moves about the boat, the muscles of upper arms and chest (please do not ask me their names—I failed my medical school entrance exams) are brought into endless play, causing breasts to lift and tilt invitingly, thereby leading to more endless play.

The best exercise below the belt is dedicated squatting and stooping. Those oriental peasants who spend their lives hand-planting rice sprouts may have round shoulders and curved spines but they all have thin thighs. Certainly better for your back and your flab, is the squat-stoop, squat-stoop, squat-stoop of any ocean passage. For milady's (or miman's) fat thighs and creeping cellulite, there is no better shedder than a sailboat.

For those males a little the other side of prime, whose chiefest muscle may have begun to display an inclination to flab (or flag), simply nothing is better than a sea voyage to reinstate the departed iron. Most sailing vessels these days are decorated by the nubilest of crewmates whose patent invitation to the ultimate iso activity only serves to shame a plumpish male into more concern for his body.

Other fats exist besides those that lie just under the skin. The fat between the ears, which on land tends to coalesce into solid bone from want of variety and excitement, and the fat that drowns and flabs your spirit from lack of challenge to that uniquely human muscle, is quickly dissipated the first time you venture into Beaufort Seven. The forty-knot winds found wandering about in Mr. B's seventh scale excite and confront both spirit and mind. If, on an ocean passage, nothing happens other than the limbering of brain and spirit, then you got your money's worth. Nothing better serves your future than a fat-free brain and a lean and hungry spirit.

Run away to sea! There will you find nature's Total Cleansing—clean air, water that does not poison, a limbering of today's body, the effortless building of new muscle, and space for mind and spirit to grow.

What the Hell more do you want?

Sailing Directions XIII

It is a straight-arrow shot west from Indonesia toward Galle (rhymes with ball) in Sri Lanka and into the caring, but slightly expensive arms of the Gauleiter of Galle, Don Windsor. He is worth every penny of what he overcharges you. You will be at home in his home and safe from the avariciousness of officials who are so stupid they don't even know what to ask for.

Sri Lanka (in healthier times known as Ceylon) is some-

times called the Perfumed Isle and sometimes the Island of Serendipity, after the Princes of Serendipity who once ruled there. The perfume you smell fifty miles at sea is a beacon of flowers and Ceylon tea. Visit Kandi, climb the mountains and buy precious carved masks and semi-precious jewels. But do not be a boor and spoil the fun by paying what is asked. Bargain with abandon, make ridiculous offers, attempt to walk away (you will not be allowed) and summon up the skills and the memory of your grandfather on Orchard Street. They will respect you for it.

14

Nothing to Wear

On land the compulsion to hide the human body behind clothing is a function of crowding and the presence of strangers. Our atomized world of billions, where there should only be hundreds, has created insecurities in us not limited to the protective hiding of our bodies. There are infinite repercussions to crowding and estrangement, some complicated and some simple. The use of clothing is the least complicated and the easiest to deal with. Take it off.

A small boat with few and intimate companions is the natural setting for nudity. Each must share bodily functions: burps, flatulence, the all-important dump—even the sounds and smells of lovemaking in the next bunk. What, under these circumstances, is more natural than throwing off the land-decreed restraint of clothing.

It is really only a sign, the last perhaps, of emancipation from non-tribal structures and strictures. While clothing serves the needs of distancing on land, at sea it is ludicrous and curiously dishonest. After weeks at sea during which you are absolutely dependent for your very life or your companions, you get to know their spirit and the truth of their nature; much more important than the shape of a breast or the hang of a cock.

Knowing a shipmate allows you to see past the mortal parts into the much more embarrassing and erotic nakedness of mind. Once you are inside someone's head, how stupid to continue to hide the body.

When we think of nudity we rarely picture a naked man. The subtle effect on men of hiding their male nakedness from each other is much more powerful and insidious than hiding women from men. Male modesty to male smacks of the fear of homosexuality and there are precious few moments on land for men to bring his fears into focus. It is the fear of focusing on another man's crotch that leads to the darkness of male guilt and confusion. At sea you deal with cock as straightforwardly as you deal with pussy. Among men it almost is possible to hear an enormous sigh of pure relief when finally they parade (and compare) before their fellow man.

Women deal with female nakedness in a much more relaxed manner. They rarely hide their bodies from each other (even though for some obscure reason locker room designers still insist on separate locker room shower stalls). The concern and the concentration with which women view another's breast or behind, is at once affectionate and clinical. Nakedness at sea for women is no confront at all. In fact, the approach of land, signalling the need to bind themselves back up into clothing, is greeted by females with universal discontent.

Nature in her wisdom intended us to view women as companions and equal helpmates first, and procreative beings second. In our modern world, until recently at least, the clothing of women is totally procreatively oriented. Clothing is designed to tempt with the hinted mysteries of the hidden parts. How much more exciting, how much more erotic is the temptation of the female mind. We get so hung up on what is hidden that getting a bra off becomes an erotic act. How dull. Piercing the filters of selectiveness of a woman's spirit is eroticism of a much higher order. Clothing creates barriers and, in sailorly terms, 'False Capes' that deceive and destroy real intimacy.

When it comes to procreative activity (screwing) it is a profound relief for women to receive a clear visual signal of a man's intentions. No shilly-shallying around, no more inane conversations ("Come here often?"), no more mixed metaphors. She knows just where she stands, and in standing out she knows just where he stands. His purpose is unmistakable.

Men finally can come out of the closet as the sexual animals their true nature dictates. They do not have to concern themselves with a line—not when they have a pennant. The final, and not inconsiderable, advantage that nakedness confers on men, bound up as they are in seams of crotch, is that it provides their growing desires with the welcome relief from painful cramping by their latest Calvin Kleins.

Being naked on a small boat with congenial companions is wonderful. If it is your male pleasure to pass the afternoon viewing callipygian delights, go right ahead. Women seem not to mind since the appraisal is not devious. Furthermore, it is a fact, never spoken about, that women are crotch-watchers. A passage surrounded by pleasant groups of emancipated dangling participles provide the women with as much pleasure as their breasts do you. There ain't nuthin' like quid pro quo!

Shed cares, shed guilt, shed family and friends who bore you. Shed banks and accountants and doctors and taxi drivers and most of all shed the damned lawyers. Shed the devious accents of land. Shed the salesmen who seek to lengthen your indenture. Shed aches and pains, shed the embarrassment of flab and shed the flab itself.

Then shed your clothes. It is, after all, the only condition in which they will allow you back into Eden.

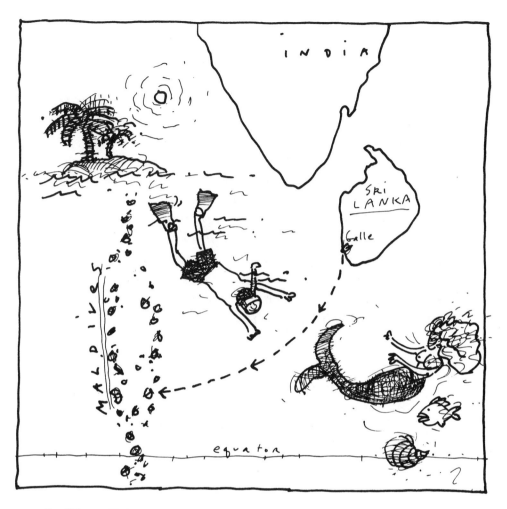

Sailing Directions XIV

*From Sri Lanka jog southwest to the Maldives. The coral
there grows live only inches below the surface of the shallow
enclosed seas that surround two thousand islands. Each island can be walked around in fifteen minutes. Most are
empty of people and of buildings and always have been so.
Most of the Maldivian islands are primeval. Check in at
Male (rhymes with dolly) buy some tortoise-shell jewelry,
cheap and illegally available, and take off for the diving of*

your dreams. If scuba is too troublesome, a snorkel is almost as good.

The Maldives are 100 percent Moslem and take their religion seriously. They are ruled by Islamic law and, among other things, liquor is forbidden. They try to be fair with westerners but they really do not like us much. Their main and only industry is tourism. While they can control the movements of the tourists they are most uncomfortable with yachts, which can come and go as they please. The government wants no disruption and sailors, being an undisciplined bunch, tend to disrupt.

Sail away from the central island as quickly as possible. Within hours you are lost in a sea of empty islands, each one a paradise of beach and palm.

15

Children Afloat

It's a damn sight better than having them aboard.

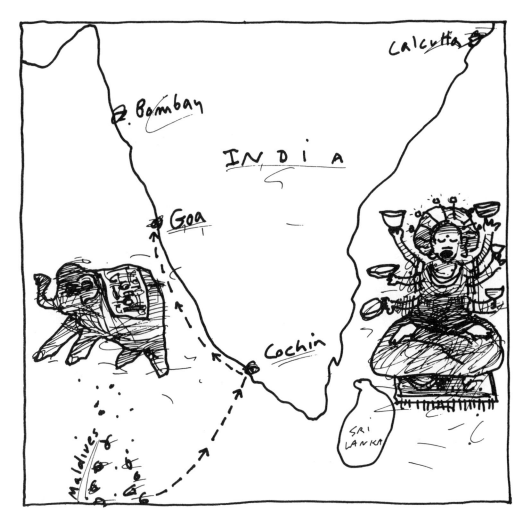

Sailing Directions XV

Northeast from the Maldives lies the wonderful womb of the world, India. Death in the streets, poverty, filth and flies and corruption. Hopeless, helpless India, where there is no better place to be, save the Galapagos. India is the teacher of souls and has been and will be for millennia. India, which the English should have left to the pashalik rule of the Princely States, lies now abandoned to a tragic parody of our industrial revolution. If you have no tears for anyone else, then cry for India.

On your way up the coast stop at Cochin, an ancient and gentle city not quite so deep in poverty as Calcutta and Bombay. Then put into Goa, where all the dreams of your youth are gathered in a community of young western refugees. They are the meagre twenty-five thousand remnant of the hippies. A gentle and harmless and loving band of young people running away from a world that had no use for them. On Wednesday afternoon, from 12 to 7, find the flea market where they all come to play. It's beautiful.

─16─

Simulating Death

On a sailboat, surrender of will (and responsibility) is even more welcome than on land. After a dark and wild watch, during which everything on the boat tried centrifugally to fly away, the moment of surrender to your relieving watch is exceeded only in delight by that second moment when, shed of clothes and concerns, you fling yourself (or are flung) into your bunk and pass out.

There are no waking hours on a sailboat when you can put aside your personal responsibility for the survival of your vessel. No one else is looking out for you. No Government, no Agency, no Corporation and no Big Brother can either help or hurt you. Your survival is your baby. Being on a boat is your ultimate way of taking your life back from these monsters. But the price you pay for control of your life is eternal vigilance. The rub is that people do not function very well in the eternal. We are beings of spurts and dashes, not constancy.

If I had been given the job of inventing man, I think I would have done things pretty much the way He did. There are a few small changes I might have made—nothing serious, mind you—just a little snipping and trimming here and there.

I might have made men a little less macho and given women a little more muscle. I might have devocalized children, at least till age three. I certainly would have given a bit more thought to teeth. I would have made dancing autonomic, like breathing. I bet that would have improved the quality of life.

Some things He did puzzle me. Appendixes, gall bladders and ear hair remain a mystery. I do, however, like pubic hair. That was a nice touch. But these are no more than a carp, 20/20 hindsight when He had to do it all on spec. All in all He was remarkably successful and demonstrated a high degree of the omniscience he lays claim to.

But until I first stepped onto a sailboat, I never could understand where He got the weird idea that each of us, all of our lives, must lie down, close our eyes and simulate death for eight hours out of each twenty-four. It was not until the first moment I was allowed to escape from the wild demands of the deck and fall onto my bunk, that the irresistible urge to "zzz" away a third of my life became no less a wondrous gift than was the gift of life itself. Indeed, on a sailboat at least, sleep is the other side of the coin of life—it makes existence possible.

After doing your sailorly duty there comes that passionately awaited moment when you are free to sleep, during which there will be not a damned thing you can do, nor are you expected to do, about the boat. It becomes totally and satisfyingly someone else's job.

On land the problems that crop up while you are asleep still are there when you awake. Problems persist, circling you like jackals at a kill. Not at sea. While you sleep the other watch is slaying the jackals and, when you awake, no problems of survival have accumulated to cloud your new day. Sailors can not carry the cares of one watch into the next.

Problems must be dealt with and solved as they arise, in the very most pressing now. Sleep is your glorious and undisturbable reward.

Although sleep is the most welcome and least harmful of morphines, it is for most of us hard to come by. Our bedrooms on land are temples to Somnus, designed to encourage and quicken his coming. The linen is tight and smooth without even one crumb to annoy us. The light can be exactly controlled and windows shielded against too much morning sun. The ambient temperature is fine-tuned. The mattress and the pillows possess just the right tone of hard/soft. And most of all there is silence to welcome sleep's onset and continuance. It is a grand wonder that with all these luxuries we ever bother to wake up.

At sea the linen, if indeed there is any, is damp and gritty and wrinkled; the light from sun or moon or those on night watch constantly is irritating; the temperature varies from peak to abyss like a stock market graph; the mattress, two inches of foam over hard board is strewn with royal peas and silence is ever murdered by the rush of water and wind and the complaining accommodation of ship to sea. Sleep at sea is patently impossible and yet, for me at least, it is easier to find and more passionately enjoyed than in the most Sybaritic of bedrooms.

I come down from my watch with every bone in my body aching from the endless kinetic battle with the boat. For four hours I have been strapped into the cockpit like Fay Wray awaiting her fate. At any moment during my watch a Kong wave could lift its head over the coaming and make imagined terrors real.

I hold tight to the boat as I rein my primal compulsion to bolt. I have no place to run—no place to hide. The comforting caves of my racial memories are closed to me. I face my adversary with no reserves. I exhaust my physical body in fighting the unpredictable movements of the boat and I exhaust my astral body in fighting down the deep implanted horror of darkness and endless sea. For four hours I remain at the most extreme limits of my capacity to survive in my body and in my head. And should the sea exert itself a bit and the winds pipe up beyond hearing, I am forced, for a time out of mind, to stretch those limits and to survive beyond them.

The release from this mind-twisting tension is either the death of your vessel (blessedly infrequent) or the total flooding warmth of being allowed, at the end of your watch, to pass on the crushing weight of responsibility. At a moment like this, both drained and fulfilled, with duty done and vessel safe, you can as easily suck in sleep as air for a yawn.

I do not dream at sea. Not only is my sleep dreamless but after standing watch through more harrowing scenarios than even my frenzied subconscious can conjure up, I have no need for nightmares. The real nightmares of the watch have been sufficient. Having tasted the metallic juices of fear for four hours on watch, I am relieved from tasting them again in my dreams. At sea you take no unsolved problems to bed with you. You have instantly solved all of life's problems, or you are forty fathoms down in a different sort of sleep.

You fall into your bunk, no matter its condition, and there is only that tiniest sliver of time before sleep rushes over you. It is then you think you hear His most distant voice saying, "Well done, well done."

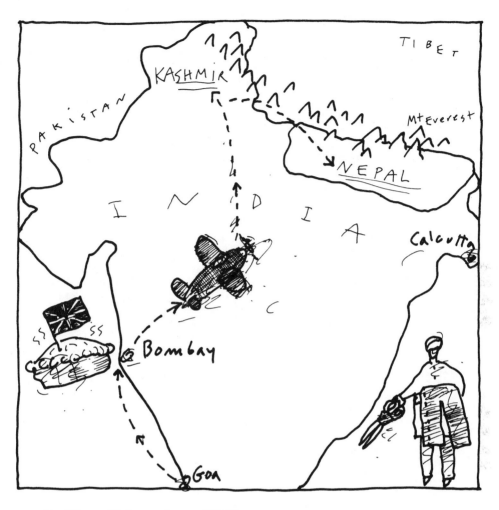

Sailing Directions XVI

Then sail north toward Bombay. Drop anchor off the Gate of India and sign in at the Royal Bombay Yacht Club. If you are lucky you can get to stay there. If not they will give you privileges at the bar and restaurant. After the fiery foods of India the bland English dishes at the Club are most welcome.

Bring samples of your best-loved clothing and have the Bombay tailors copy them for you for damn close to nothing.

115

And then get on a plane and go north to Kashmir and Nepal. Not to be missed. Your boat will be safe in Bombay if you hire a "carrier" from the Club for about a dollar a day. He will live aboard (on deck) and guard your vessel like it was the Star of India.

India's mysteries are those of men and cultures. India is the history of the world.

17

The Night Betty Dumped On My Persian Rug

We were traveling south on the Intracoastal Waterway in a new thirty-two footer. The boat had lots of room but not much flat area inside. Altogether below, there was about seven square feet of cabin sole.

On launching, my brand-new boat had received a gift from me—one square foot of precious, handwoven, Persian carpet. It was all I could afford after my final check to the builder. The carpet was my pride, exceeded only by my pride in my boat. It was the talisman of my love for her. The one square foot of carpet had a place of honor in the cabin, with two ordinary pieces of rug fore and aft to wipe one's feet before stepping on the Persian.

Betty was having a wonderful time. She never did figure out just what a sailboat was nor how it worked. North and south were a mystery to her. Many times I would come on deck during her watch only to view buoys we had passed hours before going in the other direction. She confessed to me when the trip was over that she had forgotten her glasses and could see little beyond the bow, but she never did run us aground. I will never understand why.

She is the best of companions. Funny, midwest witty and Gotham streetsmart. She sings like a nightingale, abjures alcohol as a reformed alcoholic should, beds girls as well as boys and her chiefest talent is to make everything about her beautiful. Betty loves to do two things as much as anything else in her world. Betty loves to laugh and she loves to fart.

It was this combination of laughing and farting that lead first to embarrassment and then to what was the funniest moment that ever good friends shared. It was a peal of her rollicking, uncontainable laughter that caused her to decontrol a fart and deposit a neat turd (she was wearing no clothes) on my new cabin sole, squarely in the center of my precious Persian rug.

You just had to be there.

We laughed for a week, and we still do, at an event that really had little about it that would have been acceptably funny on land. I tried to picture such a dropped turd at a gathering in my newly decorated home ashore. I could not conjure up anything but dismay, painfully embarrassed tittering, and an early departure of guests.

My small boat, on the other hand, had allowed us a moment of commonality, a round of pure human pleasure, uncorseted by the whalebones of judgment and disgust. On land one simply does not shit on somebody else's carpet. At sea you, and the boat, could not care less.

My boat continues to give me freedom, closeness, laughter and love—and the ability to see humor and warmth even in the least attractive of human activities.

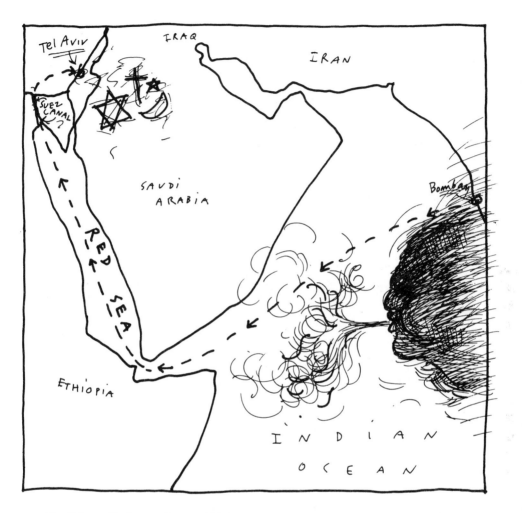

Sailing Directions XVII

From India sail westward during the northeast Monsoon. Then, only during December or January, make the impossible passage up the Red Sea. The passage up the Red Sea cannot be exaggerated in its nastiness. The wind blows mostly from perverse directions at ninety miles an hour or does not blow at all. The relatively narrow channel is beset on either side with dangerous reefs and low and invisible islands. What dangers nature has overlooked are supplied

119

by insane and passionate politics on both banks. If you survive all of this you must still contend with black freighters, heel to toe, rushing the length of that troubled Sea. An altogether good place to avoid but sailing the wrong way around the Cape of Good Hope is no fun, either. Pass through the Suez Canal—like sailing in the desert—and turn right towards Israel and the good yacht harbor at Tel Aviv. If you have sufficiently badgered the U.S. Passport office they will have given you two U.S. passports, one to be used in Israel, Taiwan and South Africa and the other in the rest of the world, which includes the crazies that do not allow traffic with the aforementioned countries.

Israel is Jerusalem, the Masada, the Galilee, the Negev, and the history of all religions past and present. Superimposed on this is the intimidating prospect of some millions of busy and clever Jews buzzing about doing what they do best—surviving!

Spend a winter and early spring in Israel until the Med warms up and then head, once again, westward.

18

Sailing Around for Free

Those crossing big oceans in small boats fight the finances of sailing and stay at sea by carefully budgeting their small hoards, and by taking work wherever and whenever it comes along.

For some reason the rich, who could easily make a comfortable and vital life for themselves on the sea, choose to stay home and make more money. Making more money rather than increasing the quality of the life you have left is incomprehensible. Putting off satisfaction, delaying the tasting of the real delights of the world for the sake of more bucks is foolish, feckless and stupid.

Besides, contrary to popular imagery, you do not need a lot of money to do a circumnavigation. Chutzpah, yes. Dollars, no.

Cruising sailors are poor in everything but spirit, adventure, vitality, purpose, health and desire. Sailors have made a good bargain with the world. We get to borrow it, play with it and be released from its deadening grip. We get to use it without owning it. What a gas!

But there still are too many who are not sailing the world

who should be. The excuse I hear most often is they can not afford to go. Only a few hundred of us are out there, scattered from Greenwich to Greenwich and from Pole to Pole. There's still lots of space in the big oceans for some congenial people, no matter how much money they do not have. Here's one pretty good idea for how to get going. The title of this piece promises a circumnavigation without money. Expand that concept and add, "and without work and without gainful employment and without skill or luck at cards." Impossible? Just watch.

First, go to your friendly banker and take out a boat loan for one year, after which you promise to repay the loan in full. Tell the banker you are buying a sailboat. The boat is his collateral. Do not tell the banker you are going to do a circumnavigation.

Locate a secondhand, well-found, blue-water-equipped sailboat produced by an American firm with an international reputation. Then contact Lloyds and buy an insurance policy good worldwide.

PROFORMA BASED ON A $100,000 LOAN

Cost of Boat	$100,000
Interest for one year	$ 12,000
Insurance for one year	$ 4,000
Cruising costs for one year	$ 10,000
Miscellaneous	$ 3,000
Your total investment is now	$130,000

Your only asset is the boat from which, within one year, you must recoup its original cost plus your expenses of $30,000.

The problem is obvious. It is the solution that is not as simple. You must now find someone, somewhere in the world, who is willing to give you a profit of $30,000 on a boat purchased in the U.S. and sailed to them somewhere in the world.

It is not possible to sail your boat to a foreign country and sell her there, where she would be worth a lot more than in the U.S. The strict and exclusionary import duties imposed by those countries where you would find eager buyers, as in Japan, prevent it. A very special place must be found where there are 1) plenty of sailors with 2) plenty of money, who are 3) familiar with and respectful of your American boat and where 4) there are no legal restrictions on its sale.

Forget about Africa, which is too poor and boasts no sailors except in South Africa, which has impossibly tight control over this kind of sale. Forget about Europe, the duties are too high. Forget about the Middle East, the Arabs don't sail and the Israelis don't have the money. Forget about South America, unless you enjoy bribing officials (a very dangerous game). India does not have a dime. China and Russia are Marxist. There, the idea of a private yacht is not even understood. Forget about Hong Kong and Singapore and Japan, where import duties will be 300% of your boat's value. Forget about Australia and New Zealand where the same holds true.

So what is left. Where in the world is a boat worth 30% more simply because you take it there and where there are no legal restrictions on its sale and where there are lots of people who desperately want to do blue-water sailing and have the means, but not the boat, to do it?

Easy. Okinawa, Guam and Diego Rivera. All these places have enormous U.S. military bases, manned by U.S. soldiers of whom, at any one time, one out of five are up for retirement. A recurring fantasy of U.S. military people is to muster out in Asia and acquire a sailboat for a leisurely cruise home. All have substantial retirement funds. Because they are Americans buying from an American, these places raise no legal barriers to yacht sales.

This is an ultimate world-class, rip-off. This is one-upping the system with style and elan. This is being rich, stinking rich, without money.

Buy a boat. Give yourself a year and sail westward to Okinawa. Sell your boat (no problem—I guarantee it). Fly home, buy another boat, go eastward this time, again to Okinawa (or Guam or Diego Rivera) and you have circumnavigated the world without a penny cost to you. If you do not believe me, invest a couple of thousand and go over yourself first to make sure the market exists. You might even make a deal, right then and there, to deliver a boat a year later.

Should you find this difficult to swallow, remember that the sea for ten thousand years and more has been the habitat of traders and merchants and privateers and capitalists and opportunists and adventurers all dedicated to taking something from A to B and realizing a profit.

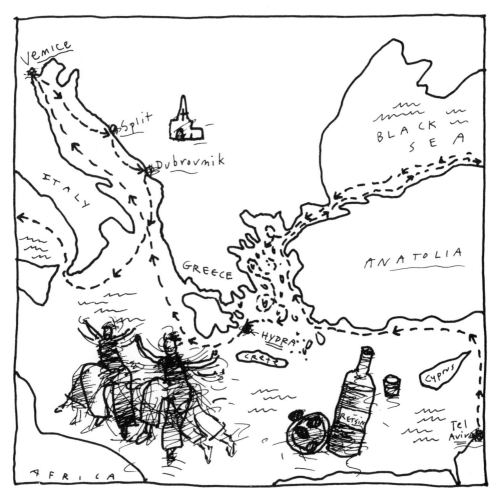

Sailing Directions XVIII

From Israel sail along the breath-taking coasts of Anatolia (the northern coast on the Black Sea is the least visited and the most wild). Then sail on to the Greek islands, where you will eat beans simmered for a week in tomatoes and olive oil, and drink wine flavored with resin to keep the Turks away. You will dance and dance until your senses leave you and you never will want to leave. The sailing in the islands is strenuous and challenging, not at all like your charters in

125

the Virgins. The seas can be steep and abusive and the Mel-tami screams at you even in harbor. When it does, hole up in Hydra and let the world go. Very nice.

Then sail up the Adriatic and enter Venice in the only acceptable way, from the sea. Take with you a copy of John Ruskin's The Stones of Venice, *from which you will learn the real history of East and West.*

Slide back down the Adriatic along the wonderful water-ing holes of Yugoslavia. Stop at Split and Dubrovnik and go inland a few miles and visit tiny churches still functioning and so ancient you can touch Christ's presence.

And then, ho hum, visit the gilded coasts of the Mediter-ranean rich.

19

Multum in Parvo

The small boat sailor suffers from a congenital inability to avoid writing about his passages. Save for this compulsion to commit pen to paper, sailors have few unifying characteristics. They are young and old, fat and thin, of all nations, of all religions and inclinations. The unifying, compelling factor driving them to write must be the sea itself, that "ineffable mystery wrapped in an enigma" on which the small boat sailor rides the winds and passes unimaginably vast distances in his small, fragile shell of a vessel.

There is something about the sea, when you are close to it, engulfed by it, threatened by it and nurtured by it, that invites feckless investigation. But as with the compelling mysteries of our time, the beginning of life, the end of God and the unfolding of physics, the questions remain too vast and the answers too small.

An early passage of mine from Bermuda to the Azores fetched me up in Horta after 22 days at sea, my longest till that time. In those 22 days I was introduced to the mystery of the sea. I unwrapped no enigmas. I solved no problems. I answered no questions. All I discovered was why the questions are so persistently asked.

The sea, although structured out of the elements and the chemicals of the inorganic world, universally is thought of as being alive. It is full of life and is composed of the very fluids of life itself. We are creatures of the sea. When our ancestors, green, slimy and not breathing too well, slithered out of the sea, they carried the chemistry of sea water in their bodies. There is little wonder that the curiosity, the interest and the empathy persists.

The mystery is life, which, as the poet said, is the only dance there is. And life in the sea presents contradictions so overwhelming that sailors of the deep seas are led by paradox to endless and, alas, fruitless comment.

On one hand is multum in parvo, the crucial importance of each small wisp of life in the sea. On the other hand is parvum in multo, the astounding paucity, the almost total absence, of life in the sea. A double paradox adding more delight than understanding to our place on the sea.

Multum in parvo—much in little. Each tiny plankton, every small fish, a bird, a smell, a wisp of wind, every least thing at sea assumes importance. Very different than on land, where we jostle and crush up against a thousand people each day, where each tree fights for its ray of sunlight against ten thousand neighbors.

On a long passage a bird is an event, a porpoise a day's entertainment, a fish a revelation. Even the weather itself changes ponderously. There is so little change and so little life (did not Aristotle say they were the same) that each small alteration and every glimpse or hint of life is seized in the mind and smelled and tasted and fondled.

To live on the sea, to stay alive on the sea, the sailor must totally immerse himself in every observation and each thin suggestion that comes his way. Is the wind dying? Increasing? Has the motion of the boat changed? Are those wispy streaks in the evening sky trying to say something? In the deep seas the small boat sailor learns very early (or does not survive not learning) of the infinite care and profound attention that must be lavished upon every stray strand of information the sea so reluctantly releases.

The living things of the sea provide the breaks, the moments of delight, the flashes of color and structure in an otherwise formless time and space. Just north of the Bermuda High (perhaps not far enough north) we lay becalmed for days, bored with our slatting sails, bored with the flat oily surface of the sea, bored with cloud patterns that seemed never to change, bored with each other and ultimately bored with the passage itself.

There was nothing to see, nothing to fasten attention to, nothing to lend perspective in either time or space. When the need for distraction had reached a palpable level, we discovered the shadow of our lifeless vessel was creating life. In the shadow of our becalmed hull, shards of life, seemingly self-generated, were pulling themselves together. Small fish appeared, then came three highdomed dolphin fish, of color so subtle they suspended belief.

Usually this ingathering can not be seen. But as a heavy calm descends in the deep oceans, the surface loses its opacity. Instead of looking at the surface, as you do when wind and waves lend it structure, you find yourself looking through the surface into the very body of the sea itself. You lie glued to a glassy sea watching intense dramas being played out beneath you. So much meaning and portent in such small structure.

In addition to the impact and importance to the sailor of all life in the oceans, you now see the other side. In this boundless sea, in this mother of all life, in its deepest reaches, there is remarkably little life. While each shard of seaborne intelligence carries a bewildering wealth of information (multum in parvo), the shards themselves are rare (parvum in multo).

The animal that pierces the veil of the surface during a calm might not be seen again in ten voyages. The flying fish that lands on your deck comes singly and silently in the night and, more often than not, slips unseen back into the sea through the scuppers. The clever and delightful pelagic fishing birds, the skimmers and the divers, are thinly spread, one bird for each square mile, perhaps, or one for ten miles or a hundred.

Whatever the figure they are scarce and each appearance is a notable, logable event. In this original spawner of life on earth, in this vast liquid mass that easily could swallow up the globe itself, the controlling axioms are "little" and "much". Paucity and multitude, coexisting in the same time and space. Not mutually exclusive, but curiously, exquisitely balanced in the deep oceans.

This is the mystery that causes sailors to write. This is the aggravating contradiction, the unreachable itch, causing them to magnify and enlarge on their brushes with the primeval source.

In a land environment senses are overwhelmed and one is forced to abstract, to select his own vision of truth from the overload. On the sea there is only one relevant image, if any at all, and God help us if we fail to pay careful and sensitive attention to it.

Like all other sailors I saw whales, porpoises and dolphins. I had flying fish land on deck. I watched unnamed clusters of platelets float by my boat. I climbed my mast and saw the long streams of seaweed herded in straight lines for miles by the wind. I saw the terrifying word "hurricane" painted in a disturbed and shattered sky.

And when I finished my passage and felt compelled to write, I realized it all had been seen by and commented on by more experienced sailors and better writers than I. But the comments are startlingly uniform.

At sea we all are the same. We all are reduced to the same reportage by the sea's plenty and paucity, but its multum and by its parvum, by the double paradox over which we sail.

Sailing Directions XIX

Early some spring, sail out from the Med through the Gates of Hercules and make the sweet rush down the trades just north of the Equator. Dip lightly into the Windward and Leeward islands of the Caribbean. By now you will be eager to get home. Drop into Antigua for a drink (and some Third World arrogance). Then sail past the over-chartered Virgins and lovely Puerto Rico, always northwards, leaving Cuba far to port, onward toward whatever port you call Home.

Home, at your ease on land away from the labor and the cares and the responsibilities of a small boat at sea. Home is the hero from the sea to accept the lauds of the never-roams. Home where you are fed and coddled and cared for and where, after a week or two of being in Heaven, you get irrationally itchy.

"Let's see now, if I leave from here and head for Bermuda then I can do that long, long Atlantic passage down around Good Hope and...."

20

The Nautical Nation

The Nautical Nation is spread around the globe on a thousand small sailboats. It is a nation of anarchists lightly pasted together by shared interests, sometimes of the most arcane nature, and by the powerful need of each of its citizens to give and receive information.

No nation can exist unless its citizens can speak to one another in a common language. A country without communication does not exist, it breaks down into small clans, each with its own language and customs. The ability to communicate freely and quickly defines the character and spirit of the constituency.

In the Nautical Nation everyone gets to share experiences and knowledge. It is like sitting around a campfire. Should a bad apple turn up it takes very little time for all to be wary. And should a sailor do something very nice or very brave, his peers sitting around their enormous campfire will quickly let him know of their approval. To facilitate this interchange, an independent postal and telephone service has sprung in the Nautical Nation, like Botticelli's Venus, full blown from the sea. As it should be in an anarchic democracy the services are free, user-created, user-operated and remarkably efficient. A sailor who knows how, can reach out for any other sailor in the world. The service broadcasts information and warnings about ports, officials, dangers and delights. What one sailor knows, all sailors know very quickly.

The telepathy is almost, but not quite, mental. The postal system is maintained in a thousand cafes and on a thousand bulletin boards in harbors all over the world. It works something like a chain letter, it transmits and magnifies the transmission at the same time. When a boat wants to reach another boat, the skipper leaves his message at any 'post office'. He requests that his message be picked up and forwarded to other bulletin boards by passing boats, who will then post and repeat the pass-along request at their next ports. Within a startlingly short time the entire Nation is involved and the message is passed quickly around the world.

There is no logic and no planning in the postal service. It works much like the description of the rider who leaped on his horse and rode off in all directions at once. It is applied anarchy.

The telephone service is Ham radio. The sailor has no better friend and no more reliable servant than his Ham radio. To operate a Ham set the sailor needs a license (free), a little acquired skill and about $500 of amateur gear. Thus equipped, and with no organization, no structure and no bureaucracy, he can speak across seas and continents for as long as he pleases at no cost. There are radio networks operated voluntarily by Hams around the world to which a sailor can reach out for succor anywhere, anytime of the day or night.

This ability to communicate independently is the cornerstone of the Nautical Nation. More and more it is possible to live on the sea with only the most tangential brushes with port. In the last twenty years a real sea life has become possible by the appearance of a few thousand small boats, manned by responsible and fiercely independent skippers—

anarchists all. This handful of boats, spread so thinly across the globe, is the critical mass that keeps the systems working. Less would be insufficient to keep the reactions going. Very much more might require the cancer of bureaucracy and thus the death of the Nation.

The Nautical Nation is the Israel of the sea. Its citizens are few, clever, cosmopolitan in outlook, inclined to be international, passionate, argumentative, iconoclastic, and only peripherally patriotic. They're very good at business and absolute masters at the fine art of survival. Like Israel, the Nautical Nation is fierce in the defense of its people and jealous of its own special way of life and, alas, also like Israel, it is awash in a sea of enemies. Like Israel, the Nation welcomes its people back, in gathering them from the diaspora of land. All are taken in, whatever they may be and wherever they may be from, just so long as they seek the sailorly life. Any sailor can become a citizen of the Nautical Nation by his own free choice.

Blue-water sailors are remarkable in their unremarkableness. They are the grey little men from a grey world and a little grey job who got lucky. They are the blessed few who by accident (which is the way the world works) have discovered the enchanting discomforts and the juicy dangers of life at sea. They are the escapees from the empty repetitive life on land, from the Big Brother society, from the expectations of folk of smaller spirit than they. They have put behind them the responsibility for idiot nuclear militarism and thus can not be taxed into guilty partnership. They are the caterpillars who underwent the Sea Change and emerged from the restrictive cocoon of their times as butterfly adventurers. At sea they become the smashers of idols, the visionaries of an alternative and a better future.

Sailors all are missionaries. They know they have reached a better life and can not resist the urge to share it. Their proselytizing weapons, however, are small and personal. Unlike the canonical shotguns of the church, the sailor uses a silent blowgun that 'whisssps' its quiet message of freedom straight to the core of our discontent and offers a cure. Sailors are too human to resist the generous impulse to bring into the fold of their own delight those who nibble hungrily on the outposts and frontiers of the Nation.

Franklin Delano Roosevelt once earned the undying hatred of the Daughters of the American Revolution by opening an address to them with the greeting, "Fellow immigrants." Those snooty ladies, burdened by overweening pride, were unwilling to admit the truth of their own origins. Wherever we live, we are all immigrants, more or less recent. In a like manner, sailors are all immigrants to the Nautical Nation.

While needful of new recruits, sailors are paradoxically resistant to large-scale immigration. They build walls of mystery at the same moment that they are passionately setting lures. Sailors are no less schizophrenic than the rest of us in our genetically directed need to exclude and include the stranger.

This siblinghood of sailors is more and less than a community. They form a tribe. They know all about each other. They have all shared the best and the worst of which the sea and each other are capable. They know the secret delight in bravery and find little need to brag or dissemble. Sailors have long since discovered that lying to non-sailors is feckless since the landbound have no way to measure the impressiveness of the deceit. There is no need to try to impress other sailors since, if you have made your passages (and it is impossible to lie about that) your colleagues already think better of you than you could ever force them to.

Within the Nation of the sea some are monohullers who believe that trimaran sailors are suicidal. Some are the solo sailors, those strange and lonely folk who wander quietly about the oceans untroubled by the tribulations of crew and companions. A very large contingent never really gets to sea. They are committed to ocean passages in principle but they are forever "getting ready" and thus avoiding the need for the real challenges of the open oceans.

If you have ever found yourself split up the middle with one foot in a dinghy and one on the dock, you will recognize the plight of that large band of sailors who yearn for the sea but who never manage to get both feet aboard. They are the part-time sailors, still paying their dues to parents and to their own procreative activity. They daysail, circumnavigate Catalina and take two weeks each year on the Chesapeake. This is the population from which the Nation replenishes itself. Some small fraction of these part-timers do break away, out into the open sea, much to their own surprise and sometimes to the dismay of family and friends who never thought they would do it. The others, like salmon who never made it to the spawning grounds, spin out their lives with no regrets save for always and forever regretting what they left undone.

You will meet citizens of the Nation all over the world. Mostly they will be hunkered down in the cheap side of any harbor, refitting, replenishing, waiting for the checks from home, arranging for crew and pursuing with concentrated dedication their newest lover-to-be. They tend to be crusty and short-tempered. All blue-water sailors take on the "I don't give a damn" attitudes of the very old. Both the very old sailors and the deep oceans have no more time or space for the things that are boring us to our death. The members of the Nation have found the paradise for which Everyman yearns. While they are willing to share it with you and even to invite you in, they are too busy eating its fruits (never the apples) to be bothered with the petulance and the pettiness of life on land.

The Nautical Nation lives. It lives in the few thousand souls who ask so little of the resources of the Earth. It lives in the handful of men and women who vastly expand their own spirits, and the universal spirit of humanness, in the strangest of all conceits—the pointless, slow, painful, dangerous and awkward process of conniving with the fickle winds to pass quietly from place to place.

Sailing Directions XX

You could do a north-to-south circumnavigation. The sailing seasons would be short and the weather unspeakable. But man has faced unspeakable conditions before and if this passage has not been done yet you can bet your bippie it will be.

From the east coast of the U.S. go up the North Atlantic through the Denmark Straits between Greenland and Iceland. Thence sail eastward, leaving the polar ice cap to port and northern Russia to starboard (talk about a rock and a hard place). Then sail south through the Bering Strait and into the Pacific for about 12,000 miles passing through Micronesia and leaving New Zealand to starboard. Then head eastward around Cape Horn, turn left and sail north to the bulge of Brazil and then northwest to home. Apsely Cherry-Garrard once wrote a book about Antarctic exploration called The Worst Journey In The World. *This one would be, too.*

21

An Epitome of Sailorly Stuff

Cruising sailors make lists like stagnant water makes mosquitoes. While some lists are useful, most are like mosquitoes, one more thing in this world we can comfortably live without.

Without the useful lists, however, we can neither comfortably live nor live at all. "Buy Lists" and "Do Lists" and "Places To Go Lists" and "Pilot Lists" (that keep you out of trouble once you get there), along with lists of articles you will never write are all a very necessary part of sailorly impedimentia. These lists are both useful and interesting.

The sense of accomplishment in list-making for nautical writers who have little to say, must approximate the pleasure of a high order orgasm. It must, or they would not continue to churn them out with such deadening regularity. The problem is that while some bits of information could be imparted via the impacted mechanism of a Victorian novel, they are most efficiently passed along in lists. What's missing is an altogether different way of disseminating nautical intelligence.

I propose using the ancient Greek practice of Epitome. An

Epitome is more than a cold listing. It is the summary form of a literary work. It is a condensation of accumulated wisdom.

Human knowledge is passed only via poetry or the novel. Since I am no versifier, and since my editor frowns upon the novelization of tiny little ideas, I find comfort in an Epitome, which opts for brevity but does not abjure style.

Here then is an Epitome of Sailing Wisdom—well, some of it anyway.

Old Urg's Secret

It was a bit early for Old Urg, but he was up to see Son of Urg off on his son's first long passage as the new master of his own many-oared long boat.

Old Urg tucked the sheepskin scroll he had carried down from his cabin more tightly under his arm and invited Son of Urg to the Great House for hot wine to ward off the chill of the morning. Old Urg had taught the young man everything he knew about navigation during the ten seasons past. He had one last gift for him, withheld till just this moment.

Son of Urg eyed the scroll hungrily, remembering the magical landfalls and the long unerring passages of his father. Old Urg had shown him how the stars and the sun and the moon could guide him across the wide oceans, how the direction and shifts of the seas hinted at far-off islands and how the winds, at certain times of the year, were like beacons in the sky.

But Son of Urg noticed how always, at the very last minute in making a port or avoiding a rocky island or coming down a narrow channel in a fog, the old man would pause, and in the heartbeat before disaster seemed inevitable, make a small adjustment to the course to carry them through.

This was the day, thought Son of Urg with glee, that the old man would reveal to him the ultimate truth, the final secret for snaking into the narrow harbors and safely making port. The secret had to come from the old Gods themselves. With that ancient mystery he, Son of Urg, would inherit the mantle of chief navigator of the clan. Pride flared and hubris lurked.

In the smoky Great House, the old man, with the dignity of a king handing his scepter of rule to his heir, handed Son of Urg the sheepskin. Son of Urg took the scroll with shaking hands and carefully, fearfully, unrolled and read the three words it contained.

"What? What? This is the secret. This is what you have withheld. This? This?"

"Yes, my son this is the final wisdom."

Son of Urg, wild with disappointment and certain this was some kind of trick or denial, read the three words aloud:

"Follow Your Nose."

Son of Urg spat incredulously, "You toy with me old man!"

He stalked out to the harbor, threw himself into his boat and beat a rapid rhythm for his rowers, so eager was he to get away from his disappointment and from Old Urg.

Old Urg's great secret was no less than the ancient art of NoseNav, which has saved my butt more times than I should like to admit. NoseNav works. It needs only a standard issue nose in reasonably good order and a string with a piece of lead on it. With these I will, and you can, make any landfall in the world.

In order to do NoseNav you need about ten days at sea before your smeller has sufficiently cleansed itself of the humors of the land. On land, importuned as your smeller is by dung and debris, it is ineffectual. At sea it becomes an amazing instrument.

I was in trouble once off the west coast of Africa. I had lost my engine and was not inclined to cross the Atlantic without power. We were just north of the Cape Verdes, but knowing that those benighted isles had little to offer, I turned east towards Senegal. I had no charts and without power the approach would be tricky, but neither did I have charts for any other entrance on the coast. Twenty miles off (we later learned) and forty miles north of Cape Verde, we smelled the Sahara. It was a hot, dry and musty smell. It could not be missed. The smell gave us our approximate longitude. As we sailed down the coast keeping the desert smell to port, we gradually picked up a different odor. As it strengthened we recognized the impacted, dense and slightly nauseating odor of too much humanity. This gave us our latitude. We were just west of Dakar, the capital of Senegal. We then threw the lead line right into port. (Well, actually we used our depth sounder but we could have used the lead and anyway it makes a tighter tale.)

There were other times, some more, some less dramatic, when we smelled our way to safety. Land always smells differently from the sea. It is hard to believe how varied and unique the odors are for different places and things. Sri Lanka smells like tea, Tahiti like flowers and even icebergs smell a bit less salty than the sea they float in.

NoseNav ain't SatNav. It's just one more of those slightly batty methods with which, since God knows when, men have found their way about great oceans.

Another is SlickNav of which TrashNav is a special case. Big boats leave a semi-permanent oil track on the water as they pass. This line in the sea is created, I think, by the slight oil leak from the bearings for their enormous propellors. It is clear enough, when you are looking for a harbor entrance still out of sight, to give you a path to follow. Of course you must be sure you are following it in and not out.

I have also observed that the big boats always leave a line of trash behind before entering harbor. TrashNav, because the trash is not continuous, is less effective than SlickNav, but it can be handy.

If there is an airport near your harbor you can, with JetNav, define its location by the coming and going of these winged sky beacons. If the geography is right, any airport is as good as any lighthouse, even better in the daytime.

PuffyNav is one of my favorites. Any blue-water sailor is aware of the high, puffy clouds that build thousands of feet atop mountainous islands. It has something to do with winds picking up moisture from the sea. As the winds are interdicted and forced upward into colder air by mountainous islands the moisture is precipitated out as cloud. At any rate, it is like an enormous tower in the sky. PuffyNav is good only in the daytime.

Not to be overlooked is EarNav, of which BangNav and TintinNav are very special cases. I once avoided losing my vessel upon exiting Okinawa one dark night by listening for the sound of the surf against an off-lying island. EarNav is most useful during fogs, when all gets very quiet. You can almost see your problems with your ears.

Under some most special circumstances BangNav, involving banging two pots together and listening for the echo, is possible. A little esoteric and crazy—but when it works, wow! what a hero you become. Can you guess what TintinNav* is all about?

Less useful, but still to be conjured with is VulcaNav (ask any volcano) and JamesWattNav, which involves detecting and following into harbor the pollution being dumped into the sea therefrom.

---

* Hint. "The Tintinabulation of the Bells, Bells, Bells."

JamesWattNav is not so silly as it sounds. I once located my position off the mouth of the Yangtze by noting the sharp division between the clear green ocean and the polluted, bright yellow river. I then crossed that line at a right angle and simply followed the shit up the Yangtze to the Wang Poo, where I turned left to Shanghai.

When all these sophisticated Nav methods do not apply, you can always resort to less elegant and more expensive systems, such as radar, loran, satellites and, Heaven forbid, your sextant. Real salty old sailors thumb their noses to all that mechanical nonsense and do not lose their boats any more (nor, I must add, any less) than electric sailors do.

Oh yes, back to Son of Urg. Eleven days out from harbor, after sundown, his vessel struck an iceberg he had failed to smell and was lost with all hands.

Sailorly Foods

Sailorly foods have a number of shared characteristics. They all keep for a very long time and when they spoil they go gracefully and without mess. They are pithy and succinct and do their nutritional job with elegance and little waste. Because your nose, after a few days at sea, will reach a new plateau of efficiency, sailorly foods are light and subtle in odor, both in the cooking and in the eating. They are cheap, universally available and cookable in a hundred gentle ways.

Food at sea must be natural. Your body, after starting a sea change of cleansing the poisons of the land, will reject preservatives and artificiality and will reach out for purity and simplicity. Come to think about it, sailorly foods are the way people should eat on land, too.

Fish. Anything you pull over the gunwale in the deep oceans is edible. Poisonous fish are denizens of reef and shallows, where the sea is crowded and where piscine defenses have developed high tech forms. The continental shelves are where man is storing his wastes. In the deep oceans fish have never learned to be mean. They exist as the universal food for each other and for you.

Pasta. Keeps forever. Easy to cook. Totally non-abusive to the belly and great for old teeth. Cheap and accepting of any sauce.

Rice. Same as Pasta. The ubiquitous food of the East. Available anywhere and, like pasta, accepting of any sauce. Do not buy rice in Sri Lanka. The grocers in that land lace it with fine white chips of unremovable sand (bad for teeth of any age) to increase the weight.

Other Grains. In fact, all grains are sailorly. Cold cereal, hot cereal, beans, (not exactly grains, but close) and popcorn all are successful foods. Cold cereal requires milk, not always available, but my daughter eats hers with pineapple (!) juice.

Eggs. Perfect. Last for months unrefrigerated and longer in the cold. (A Bad Egg is not just an expression, so be careful.) A google of uses.

Milk. In sterilized or powdered form, this is the only sailorly food that has allowed itself to be successfully tampered with.

Bread and Crackers. Necessary stuff but there are problems. Bread is tedious to make and crackers get soggy. Seal and carry crackers and put up with the heat in the galley for bread. Use bread as a treat food, do not serve it everyday.

Like sex, it will be most appreciated in its occasional, rather than its continual presence.

Fruit. Nothing is more yearned after on a passage. Buy bananas by the stalk, very green and watch them go ripe row by row each day. On my boat in the early stage of a passage, we punish wrongdoers by depriving them of their daily banana. As ripening accelerates and supply exceeds demand, the punishment becomes two bananas. Oranges go bad quickly but are worth the trouble. Lemons last much longer and those hard little limes go on forever.

Veggies. Lay in great stocks of onions and potatoes. Especially onions. Get them where they are cheap and buy too many. You can't. Cabbage is one of the few long-lasting green vegetables and as such deserves consideration. It is a little ripe in the cooking and does smell up the boat, but is Oh So welcome after a few weeks at sea.

That's it. You need no more. More would be less.

Approach-Avoidance in Nautical Alimentation

Here are not the usual lists of vittles and supplies and the tactics of storing, preserving and preparing them, but a basic strategy for alimentary management that was paid for by me in the coin of nausea. Whatever alimentation is not discussed herein, you may approach, but with temerity. All else avoid with enthusiasm.

The title, admittedly, is a bit overstructured. But since we live at a time when people seek predigested and highly systematic solutions, it seems to fit. For those of you who see through the bullshit I offer the title "Eating & Vomiting At Sea."

1. Avoid all pastry. Pastry, like no see-ums, is one of God's little errors, adding nothing to man's well-being, much to his waistline and in tummies already under siege, raises the level of attack. Pastry requires heating up the galley (counterproductive in the tropics), uses up lots of fuel and rarely stays edible beyond its day of creation. If you are not in France, where pastry may well be worth the sacrifice, the stuff you buy will be larded with pig fat, half baked and full of dead insects. It has only one redeeming characteristic. It is uneatable.

2. Avoid finishing the food that is served you. It is likely that the mal will descend upon you not in the beginning of your meal but at some point well along when your belly starts feeling put upon. In avoiding seasickness, the quantity of food eaten is just as important as is quality and kind. It should be self-evident that, even on land, too much food leads to discomfort. Eat little, eat frequently and never, never mop up your plate—that is where the grease is.

3. Avoid dehydration. Drink lots of water even if at first it makes you a little nauseous. Experiential observations (the only kind that mean anything) demonstrate that as the belly gets abused by motion it starts to generate acid. Drinking water dilutes these acids and reduces the discomfort. When you do whoopsy, the lower concentration of acid is easier to pass and won't leach out the enamel in your teeth.

4. Never, never eat before taking to your bunk. Think about it. There you lie in a bed that seems to be moving in all directions at once. If you have just eaten, all that stuff is

slopping around in your already confused gut. When you are vertical some of this internal ebb and flow can be controlled, but when stretched out, you are no more than an interior beach upon which wave after wave of nausea breaks.

5. Avoid tobacco, alcohol, dope and other chemical excitants. The sea is exciting enough. Taking control of your belly is a process of dimming it down, not lighting it up. As your palate clears, as it will after a week or two at sea, the simplest of foods will hold new adventure. Tobacco and dope distort and cloud the palate and alcohol causes you to fall overboard. Avoid crew who smoke. There is nothing more disgusting than to come below after some hours in the cleanest air left on this planet, only to be faced with vapors of carcinogens and the decaying remnants of a thousand cigarettes embedded in your upholstery. If you should find yourself at the beginning of a long passage with a crewmate who smokes, throw his stash overboard. He may kill you but it will be worth it.

6. Avoid meat. There is something curiously contradictory about eating meat at sea. You left the land to put meat eating and other abusive practices behind and now you find yourself dragging some of the rotting stuff along. Whether it is canned, dried or fresh (that is, in the process of spoiling) there is no way to esthetically keep it aboard. Meat is too eloquent, too evocative a food, especially since your belly needs simplicity not succulence. Besides, the heavy smell of cooked meat lasts far beyond its first pleasant whiff on the grill.

As if all this were not distasteful enough, the literature of the sea is loaded with descriptions of maggot-infested meat. We may have banished the maggots but we have not excised their image. The whole subject of meat is just too damned unpleasant. Deny meat. Eat sailorly foods.

7. Avoid avoiding regurgitation. Your body knows its needs better than you. Any conscious attempt to interfere with the

intolerable urge to throw up will only worsen matters. The scenario is familiar: you are stretched out on your bunk exhausted from your last trip to lee a few moments earlier. You are crushed to feel your gorge once again start its ascent. You know there is nothing left to contribute, but your body insists. Throwing up is one of the most physically exhausting activities and you have been at it for hours, maybe days. You return from this useless, final trip to lee white, shaken and clammy and you fall on your bunk and into blessed, curing sleep. Emptiness of the belly does not nor ever will relieve seasickness, but exhaustion does it every time! You must allow your body to exhaust itself. You must give in to the violence of vomiting. Nothing cures the mal like the sleep of exhaustion.

8. Never avoid voiding. In some mysterious manner, hidden in the slime of evolution, your bowel bone is connected to your belly bone and your belly bone is connected to your gorge bone. Relieving one end of the tube remits some distress at the other end. A seasick body yearns for emptiness and does not much care from which end it comes.

Bowel movements and vomiting are subjects that evoke laughter and embarrassed titters in some circles. They are, however, deadly serious matters on a small sailboat, matters that may make or destroy a passage. Should your sensibilities be so finely honed as to be repulsed by these most universal of human activities, then my advice to you is: Do Not Sail.

9. Approach garlic with care. It is almost impossible to find the strength of purpose to totally avoid this ebullient spice. Garlic is life in food and when you go cold turkey, the pain may not be worth the advantages gained. The problem with garlic is not that it produces garlic breath. All those aboard get that and thus no one notices each others' vapors. The real problem is the subtle and differing chemistry garlic plays with the smell of our skin. It varies for each of us so that, unlike breath, we can all smell each other while unaware of

our own offense. The skin odor is strong and lasts for varying lengths of time in different individuals. Your whole crew may shed it in a day save one poor soul, who, outcast and not knowing why, reeks for a week. Try a bit and see what problems emerge. Set up a 'smell drill' for a few days and smell each other regularly to determine the bearable level of tolerance. Or make offending persons live on deck and to lee for a week. But that is draconian. Ask me, I know.

10. There is no greater truth in dealing with seasickness than work will set you free. Do your job. Stand watch even when you know it is impossible. Take a turn in the galley, even if you retch at the mere thought of food. Do your share then do more than your share. Exhaust yourself in your duties, defeat the mal with physical labor and, as a bonus, gain the love and respect of your mates. They have been through it and know what you are suffering. You are not alone. They have all been there, again and again and tomorrow yet once more.

11. A cure? Sure. A dollop of scopalomine behind the ear. Works like magic.

Toidy Training

A marine head is a straightforward device. It pumps ocean water in, mixes it with waste and pumps it out again. Nothing could be simpler. Nothing is more foolproof. Nothing on a boat incorporates more decades of engineering experience. And nothing is more consistently troublesome.

The care and feeding of your indispensable marine head is based on four cardinal, absolutely inviolable rules. A kind of adult toidy training.

1) When not in use always keep the lid down. On land we use our toilets as wastebaskets. At sea the unconscious act of tossing anything into the can leads to trouble. Your bathroom at home tends not to leap around. At sea, all sorts of objects are accidentally thrown in, from bottles of shampoo (no disaster unless the cap comes off) to bobby pins (disaster! get out the tools).

So keep the lid down, it may just save you from the worst job in the world.

2) Waste matter is the altered form of food. You are no more than a long tube. Into one end stuff is pushed and, out of the other end that stuff, in an altered state, is evacuated. If you keep firmly in mind that the marine variation of Mr. Crapper's invention, unlike the one in your bathroom, will accept only altered state material, you will, at least anally, be a more successful sailor.

The only stuff that can go into a marine head is that stuff you have previously put into your own head. For those of you with literal rather than literary minds, picture your marine head as a contiguous extension of your asshole and you will never have any plumbing trouble on board.

3) I spent a good deal of time in India where evacuation is most uncomplicated and cleanliness is a matter of survival. The Indians, all half a billion of them, use no toilet paper. It is too expensive and considered unsanitary. Their solution is to wash themselves with water. This is a perfect solution onboard since most plumbing troubles there are the result of too damn much toilet paper. Post-dump washing saves the cost of the paper, promotes sanitation and health and does not antagonize your toilet.

I do not expect to wipe out a lifetime habit with a piece of lore from another culture, even though it is the perfect alternative. At best you now know there are alternatives to toilet paper. (The Indians also think that blowing your nose into a piece of cloth and then stuffing it into your pocket is disgusting.)

One step removed from the Indian Solution is the method we enforce on our boat. We use toilet paper but insist that each scrap be carefully kept and immediately thrown overboard (to lee, please, to lee) after each trip to the head. It works wonderfully well.

So throw away the toilet paper and wash with water. If you can not deal with the blinding elegance of that solution, then enforce the "used toilet tissue to lee" edict. Either will work and in the long run both will encourage regularity, a condition much to be desired.

4) After each (and every) use of your marine head give it a generous dollop of bleach. This will keep the bowl unstained and it will work itself into the pumps and valves and other innards of your head and keep them sweet, too. Should a well-bleached head need disassembly, the job will be much less repugnant than one that has not been so treated. Each and every means each and every. Skip not even one use. Concerning this function you must indeed become anal compulsive and to hell with Freudians.

How to Sleep on a Sailboat

If you can sleep with water dripping into your ear, on a hard bed that has just been dropped from an airplane in a raging storm, you need read no further. If, on the other hand, your sleep muscle is as tender and underdeveloped as is mine, and needs all the help it can get—then read on.

1) Most important. Air your linen every day. Let it whip about in sun and wind to rid all the true grit, along with some of the salt and wrinkles. Miss not one day's airing and miss not one night's sleep.

2) Do not go to sea without fitted sheets. Call me spoiled, sissified and effete, but I will continue to maintain that fitted sheets add more pure physical pleasure to a passage than all of the studied luxuries of Bill Buckley's *Cyrano*. Have a couple of sets made up. If you cannot afford them, sell one of your SatNavs. No sacrifice is too great.

3) Unlike tight shoes, tight bunks are wonderful. Arrange yours so you have plenty of length but just barely enough width. Trying to sleep while holding first the port and then the starboard side of your bunk simply does not work. In order to sleep on a gyrating sailboat you must immobilize yourself. Wedge yourself in so not even your belly can find the space to slop sickeningly.

4) The skipper's best soporific is a telltale compass, hung above his bunk and read from its bottom side. Just cracking an eye reassures him that the boat is going approximately where it is supposed to go.

5) Except when you are at sea, where they don't exist,

mosquitoes murder sleep on a boat. While in port learn to sleep with at least a sheet, never without some cover, and learn to enclose yourself so that the last mosquito, which you could not find, will eat its own heart out rather than yours. On any of your parts that must remain exposed, use insect repellant liberally. It is little known that the repellant action is due to the fact that upon application your skin becomes slippery and unpleasant to the mosquito's feet. The repellant action is physical not chemical. It might cost you a little loving but you can make that up at sea.

6) Mount small 12-volt oscillating fans above each bunk. They use little power and the movement of even hot air simulates coolness. Besides, they have a nice reassuring hum, like a Mommy, or the Johnny Carson Show.

7) It is extremely difficult to sleep with cold water dripping into your ear. You will find, no matter what boat you are on or what bunk you choose, or what position you take in your bunk, that water will drip in your ear. There is some, as yet uninvestigated, relationship between ears and water. The responsible skipper will see to it that his crew's sleep is not watered down. But deck leaks are subtle. They usually originate yards away from where they appear and they are aggravatingly intermittent. The detective work required to track down sleep-drowning drips can take weeks, sometimes years. There is nothing, however, that you can do on a boat that is more worth the effort.

8) The only kind of blanket to use next to your skin is one of light cotton flannel. They are delicious, soothing and as soft as a baby's ass. Try flannel sheets. They are the black satin of the sailing world.

9) If you still sleep with a Teddy Bear or your own blanky, take it along. At sea nobody will laugh.

10) The last word on sleep, in case you now are frightened by the specter of long nights of sweaty tossing and turning

is: forget it. The first time you hit the sack at the start of a serious passage you will sleep like a Pharaoh. And you'll be almost as difficult to awaken.

A Zennish Look at Sailing

Sailing schools obfuscate. They have little to teach (sailing being an autonomic activity), so they are decked out with complicated systems, arcane language and exhausting detail that serves only to make sailing more complicated than it is. They are characterized by long passages, expensive tutoring and involved curricula. Self-serving cow droppings!

Plato defined a school as a log with a pupil at one end and a teacher at the other. All you need to learn to sail is a day-sailer with a student at one end and a teacher, either asleep or absent, at the other.

The less the teacher interferes with your journey into the heart of the matter, the better. The less he teaches the more you learn. The more peripheral mysteries he excludes the faster you get to the central, enlightening mysteries.

ZenSail is a non-Western, non-linear method of learning to sail. It is instinctual rather than intellectual, reactive rather than rational, self-taught, inward-directed and automatic. The lone precondition is that the novice empty his mind. An empty cup fills more easily than a full one.

ZenSail requires six Rings (pieces) of information that must become part of the being of the novice. When needed, the information leaps, unbidden, out of mind. This information moves the novice into realms of instinct, feeling and belief and urges the merging of mind with muscle. ZenSail does not make a sailor. To be a sailor one must do sailing. Knowledge of the construction of his vessel and theories of sail cause clutter and confusion. The novice has no need to know how things work or why they work. The legitimate goal of the novice is to learn what to do in order to sail.

The First Ring informs the sailor that he must be continually and endlessly aware of the direction of the wind relative to his boat. The wind can change direction, the boat can change direction or they both can change direction relative to each other.

Every sense must be honed to provide the sailor with an uninterrupted flow of information about the wind. If awareness of the wind's direction is lost, even momentarily, there is no way to sail. Sailing is the wind and only by knowing the wind's direction are we able to move and guide a vessel.

Sight, touch, smell and hearing all attend to the wind. Watch the changing shape of the sails or see a piece of ribbon tied to a stay. Become aware of the hull's noise as it pushes through the water. Feel the altered pressure on the tiller. Listen for new tunes resonating in the rigging. Smell the nearness of land that causes changes in wind and sea. The inner ear, that mysterious and hidden balancing act in our heads, senses when the vessel is leaning more or leaning less in response to the swing and pressure of the wind.

The next three Rings relate the direction of the wind to the direction the sailor wants to go. Remember this: The direction of the wind is nature's gift, the course the sailor's choice. The boat moves when the boom is at the correct angle to the direction of the wind. That is all there is.

The Second Ring deals with a wind coming from the front of the boat. If the sailor wants to go in the direction from which the wind is blowing (against the wind), he brings the boom in close to the centerline (from bow to stern) of his boat. The boat then moves as in Drawing A.

The Third Ring deals with a wind coming from the side of the boat. If the sailor wants to go at right angles to the wind (alongside the wind), he places the boom at a moderate angle to the boat's centerline. The boat then moves as in Drawing B.

The Fourth Ring deals with a wind coming from the back of the boat. If the sailor wants to go in the same direction as the wind (with the wind), he places the boom at a large angle to the centerline. The boat then moves as in Drawing C.

The Fifth Ring describes the way a sailboat can be made to go against the wind, arriving at a position that lies directly into the wind, although it can not be made to sail there in a straight line. Aim the boat a little to the left of the wind (and your destination), putting the boat in the condition of the Second Ring, sail a bit, then turn the boat a little to the right of the wind and again apply the Second Ring. The boat will arrive at a point that is directly into the wind, as if it had sailed in that direction. See Drawing D.

The Sixth Ring describes the way a sailboat can be made to go directly with the wind safely and without difficulty. Aim the back of the boat slightly to the left of the following wind (Fourth Ring), sail a bit, then aim the back of the boat a little to the right of the following wind (Fourth Ring). The boat will arrive at a point that is directly away from the wind. See Drawing E. (A caveat, the only caveat: when the wind is from the back of the boat the boom can swing over very quickly. Keep your head down.)

A novice should be able to move his boat in any direction after a few minutes' practice. Ten additional minutes of hands-on training from an experienced sailor will be helpful, but no more information is required. The novice will then spend the rest of his life becoming a sailor.

Choose a day with a gentle breeze, locate a reasonably

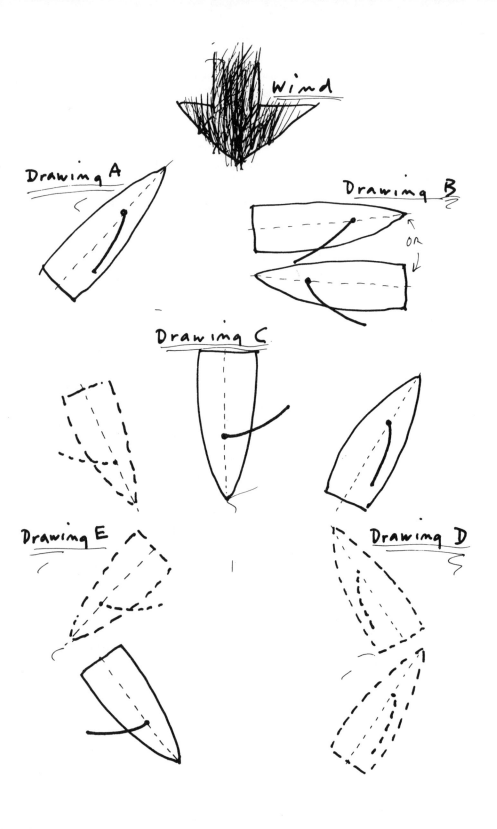

Wind

Drawing A

Drawing B

OR

Drawing C

Drawing D

Drawing E

deep body of water so you will not go aground. Rent a keel boat of about twenty feet in length and follow the simple rules of ZenSail. The novice will soon be taking her where he wants her to go. On the way home he is allowed to buy a cute sailor's cap.

— Epilogue —

Angels in the Rigging

On those quiet nights when there is just enough breeze to hold the sails from slatting and barely enough to move the hull through an oily sea, there arises, from the region of my top set of spreaders, the faintest hint of disputation.

While the voices of the subjects under contention lie beyond the threshold of hearing, their subsensate sounds seem to be the muted voices of gentle and good-natured friends in the most mild disagreement over how best to achieve some unanimously sought-after goal.

Should the winds start rising, or the seas signal a coming disorder, or should an unexpected light lift over a distant horizon, or should any untoward event present itself, the conversational comity disappears, and in its place an umbrella of protection spreads over my little ship.

When I first read the description of the visits by the Great Navigator himself during Slocum's long and lonesome passages, I dismissed the scene as a bit of dramatic license by an old salt, or, more likely, a touch of sun-induced delirium. Slocum, I decided, really believed Columbus was in the cockpit, his fine Italian hand on the tiller, guiding the exhausted Josiah through the bad places. A moment of relief for the old sailor to sense companionship and assistance in the midst of a vast, unfeeling sea. A figment, certainly.

I am no longer sure. I no longer dismiss presence. If I can have nine seraphic busybodies living in my rigging, why could not Slocum have old Chris Columbo in his.

In my salad days, more sure of myself than now, my response to arguments extra-physical was, "Prove that it is." Now when someone challenges a bit of my own personal psychic comfort, I answer with a shrug, "Prove that it isn't." I am no longer concerned with whether a thing is or is not. I am more concerned with how it feels. And having nine angels living in my rigging feels just fine.

Some years after my fifth decade I was made aware that it is entirely possible (prove that it isn't!) to receive a gift of angels. Until that time, walking the narrow line of rationalism, I neither believed in angels nor in the ability of one mortal to award them to another. Always demanding touch-ability, I rendered much to Caesar and little or nothing to the Other Guy, who, assuming one of the less attractive of mortal attitudes, became jealous and insinuated a lady into my life. Her arrival was good for me, passably good for the lady and wonderful for the Other Guy who finally got rendered his portion.

The lady was no more "real" than the angels she bequeathed me. Where I saw one world she saw a thousand; where I saw one flower she saw a bouquet and where I saw a pebble she saw the whole blinding totality of God's work. I lived in a Flatland of feeling and belief. She rotated me ninety degrees. She brought me in out of the cold.

The gift of the angels came when she decided that her ardor for sailing, and I expect, pour moi, waned. She announced that she would no longer be passage-making with me, but that she was doubtful about my ability to survive without her. She had spent a good part of her time aboard mending and bandaging the various gouges, burns and breaks dealt to me by the playfulness of my vessel and my own clumsy incaution. The lady was sure that, without her to look after me, I would quickly succumb to trauma and carelessness. She was not the only one distressed at my being cast off to look after myself. I also became infected by her dim view of my future. The prognosis, she declared, was awful.

She pondered the problem and arrived at, what was for her, a logical solution. If she could not be there to look after me then she would assign a sorority of her personal guardian angels to mount watch over me.

And so it came about that my twittery, chattery little assemblage of winged putti set up housekeeping aloft. There they live, needing no sleep, never tiring and ever alert for the dangers that beset.

They whisper calming thoughts to the winds and sing lullabies to the seas, they cause lightning to veer ever so slightly and reefs to loudly announce their presence. They police the deck for weaknesses and, with angelic little snorkels, they check from waterline to keel. And should they find something amiss, they set up disquieting, subliminal signals in my head. They never speak directly to me (and come to think of it, neither did the lady) but I know they are there.

Much hurt and agony was avoided. Near misses became a way of life and the fame of our little vessel spread over the South China Sea. We were the lucky boat. Typhoons died in our path like tutued swans on the stage of the Met. Great seas bearing down upon us from opposite directions met in synchrony rather than in disorder and plussed and minused each other into gentle billows. Pathways through the reefs opened like the Red Sea for Moses and some of us aboard were not even Jewish.

As our fame grew so did suspicion. Others, always eager to validate their bad luck by invidious comparison, greened at our good fortune. Not all were jealous, but some were. As we entered a harbor, those boats eager to share in our luck would rub up against us purring like hungry cats, while others, the skeptics and the naysayers, would disdainfully lift their Victorian skirts and edge away, as if the sulphurous smell of Belial was upon us. They were sure we had made a pact with the Devil.

But my thrice three seraphim ignored it all and went about their appointed task. "Look after *Unlikely VII*," they had been exhorted, and with seraphic singlemindedness, like cats watching a mousehole, they mounted watch. Neither curiosity nor jealousy nor adulation affected them until one hot Sunday when we sailed into the island of Bikalkilunni, in the Republic of the Maldives and dropped anchor next to a black steel cutter, a mean and serious looking boat called *Vroon*.

Vroon was sailed by a passionate Slav with a prodigious thirst, and a woman of shattering beauty, three inches taller than I, lighter haired, a dark-skinned, half-Russian baroness, half Herzogovinian peasant and half witch.

The instant our anchor rode rattled through the hawse, my angels went silent. No chatter, no twitters, and for a moment the envelope of care was breached. I closed my eyes and reached for them in my mind. I sensed dismay, nervousness and the compulsive need to be away, far away from the black cutter.

I wanted to stay. The place was beautiful, the diving was endless discovery. The coral was untouched and grew alive to within inches of the quiet surface. There are two thousand islands in the Maldives and my boat strained to be at any but the one I was at. I tried, but neither the beauty of the tall woman nor the charm of the Slav, nor the coral, nor the sunsets, nor the lost paradise of the place could resist the strident cry of "Sail Away!"

So sail away I did, leaving a woman I wanted and a place

to which I could never return. I listened to the silent shrieks from high in the shrouds and departed.

It was not until half a year later and half a thousand miles away that the tale was finally told. The tall woman suddenly appeared to me in Bombay out of a fog. I gleefully scooped her up and was taught again that eventuality often exceeds fantasy. She led me down the darkest streets and up darker alleyways where we shared the long pipes of the vapors of escape.

In the midst of these clouds of bemusement, she told the story of the *Vroon*. After two years, her man had turned against her and, in desperation, she had sought out one of the Shaman who keep voodoo alive in those distant islands. She told me that the Shaman had discovered JuJu vials, filled with evil spirits, which someone, meaning her harm, had scattered throughout the black cutter. She told me how she had fled, half naked and terrified, from the *Vroon*.

She believed and my angels believed and shared the terror of the tall lady as they hustled me away from the black cutter which, some say, came to grief and took others with her.

As with most human events, and all extra-human ones, everything finally comes down to belief. My lady believed in her angels. The tall woman believed in the JuJu. My angels believed in the JuJu and in the imperative need to be away from them, although I have trouble believing in the JuJu since it is more comfortable believing in angels than in ghouls. My seraphim I stick by. They have proved themselves to me too many times to be rewarded with agnostos and disrespect.

Hear them on quiet nights and feel the excitement when their friend and confidant the porpoise appears. Evidence to convince the most committed cynic that Belief exists, God lives and Angels twitter.

More Books for the Cruising Sailor

There Be No Dragons
by Reese Palley

"...a delightful blend of information and stories, with emphasis on the human aspect of sailing. Witty, irreverent, and inspirational with as much 'why to' as 'how to'." *Cruising World*

Advice to the Sealorn
by Herb Payson

"Payson covers a broad range of cruising topics in an informative and often entertaining manner. Whether planning to extend your cruises or live aboard, this is good reading." *Cruising World*

The Great Cruising Cookbook
by John C. Payne

Over 350 recipes collected from the author's travels around the world. Special attention is given to the unique needs of cruising sailors, including rough weather foods, worldwide provisioning and a professional approach to galley equipment.

Tamata and the Alliance
Bernard Moitessier
Translated by William Rodarmor

Moitessier became famous for his daring sailing exploits, often done solo. This fascinating memoir spans the time from Moitessier's magic childhood in Indochina to the months before his death in June 1994. A memorable story of an exciting life.

Blown Away
by Herb Payson

Herb and Nancy Payson and their large brood of teenage children cruise the Pacific for six and a half years. "A realistic portrait of an adventurous, enterprising family, with enough sailing lore to satisfy most bluewater buffs." *Publishers Weekly*

By Way of the Wind
by Jim Moore

The adventure begins when Jim Moore announces to his bride of two months that they will build a boat and sail to the South Pacific. "The best sailboat cruising book to come out in a long time." *Washington Post*

Sheridan House
America's Favorite Sailing Books